Usborne Battlegame Books
GALACTIC WAR

ANDREW McNEIL

Acknowledgements
We wish to thank the following individuals and organizations for their assistance and for making available material in their collections.

British Interplanetary Society
Cornell University
Mansell Collection
Mary Evans Picture Library
Rockwell International

'Deadly Planet' devised by James Opie.
'Galactic War' and 'Space Pirates' devised by Dave Rotor.

Illustrators
Stephen Bennett
Gordon C. Davies
Brian Lewis
John Marshall
Michael Roffe

Additional artwork by
Chris Lyon
Guy Smith

© 1991, 1976 Usborne Publishing Ltd.

The name Usborne and the device ⚁ are Trade Marks of Usborne publishing Ltd. All rights reserved. No part of this publication may be reproduced, stored in a retrieval system or transmitted in any form or by any means, electronic, mechanical, photocopying, recording or otherwise without the prior permission of the publisher.

First published in 1975 by
Usborne Publishing Ltd,
Usborne House, 83-85
Saffron Hill, London EC1N
8RT, England.

This edition first published in 1991.

▼ **A.D.2076.** Space prospectors hunt for minerals on the rocky surface of Vesta. At 540km (335 miles) across, this is the third largest body in the Asteroid Belt between Mars and Jupiter. On the left a spacecraft, loaded with ore samples, blasts off for Earth.

Art and editorial direction
David Jefferis
Text editors
Tony Allan
Margaret Chester
Rules editor
James Opie
Technical advisor
Kenneth Gatland
Picture researcher
Caroline Lucas

ABOUT THIS BOOK

Galactic War explores the future. It includes pull-out boards, cut-out pieces and rules for four new games set in the 21st century and beyond.

Starting from what we already know of the Universe, the book speculates about things yet to come. Space cities in orbit between Earth and the Moon. Humanoid creatures with independent brains filling the gap between men and machines. The mysteries of hyperspace, where neither time nor distance exists, and of the 'black holes' which may lead into it.

The games include 'Invasion Earth!' in which Earth forces track down aliens breeding in the Pacific Ocean, and a struggle for survival on a 'Deadly Planet'. In 'Space Pirates' rival prospectors race to bring valuable minerals back to Earth from the Asteroid Belt. The title game pits the might of the Stellar Federation against invaders of the Galaxy.

CONTENTS

- 4 Introducing the Solar System
- 6 Into infinity
- 8 Pioneers who showed the way to the stars
- 10 Robot explorers
- 12 Surviving in space
- 14 Space shuttles and space cities

Pull-out section
Boards and pieces for four battle-games: Space Pirates; Deadly Planet; Invasion Earth! and Galactic War

- 16 Timechart
     Improving and storing the game pieces
- 17 Rules for the battlegames
- 21 The wealth above our heads
- 22 Voyage to the stars
- 24 Alien life
- 26 The far future
- 28 Index

INTRODUCING THE SOLAR SYSTEM

The planet Earth is part of the Solar System. Solar means "belonging to the Sun". The Sun's system includes nine planets, 60 satellites or moons, thousands of minor planets or asteroids, and many comets, meteors and meteorites.

Ball of fire

The centre of the Solar System is the Sun. The Sun is a star, one of billions in the Galaxy. It is a giant ball of gases, mainly hydrogen and helium. These gases are the Sun's fuel, and they react like a continuous H-bomb explosion to produce tremendous heat and light. On the surface of the Sun, which is called the photosphere, meaning "ball of light", patches of cooler gas show up as dark sun spots. Sometimes material in the Sun's thin atmosphere condenses into huge prominences which arch above the surface or shoot out like flames.

Although the Sun is very hot, burning at about 15 million°C at the centre, and very large compared with Earth, it is really a very ordinary star.

The nearest planet to the Sun is Mercury. Photographs taken by the Mariner 10 space probe show that its surface is covered with craters, like the Moon's.

Life is possible on Earth because it is just the right distance from the Sun. If it was any nearer, the water needed for most life would boil away. If it was further away it would freeze. Although the heat which radiates from the Sun is very great the Earth's atmosphere filters it and makes it tolerable.

The Earth and its neighbours

The Earth revolves round the Sun in 365¼ days and rotates once every 23 hours, 56 minutes and 4 seconds. These are our planet's years and days.

The two planets nearest the Earth are Mars and Venus. At one time it was thought that there might be life on them. Modern space probes have shown this to be unlikely. Venus, which is nearer to the Sun, is the nearest planet in size to Earth. It is very different on the surface, because a thick atmosphere of carbon dioxide traps the heat of the Sun. At the surface the temperature is 460°C – as hot as the top of a blast furnace. Mars is about half the size of Earth, and is further away from the Sun. Space probes show that it is mainly desert. On its surface the air is very thin – about the same as the atmosphere on top of Mount Everest on Earth.

Giants of the Solar System

Beyond Mars is the largest and most interesting planet in the Solar System, Jupiter. It has a diameter eleven times that of Earth. It has a very strong magnetic field and sends out radio waves which can be picked up on Earth.

Saturn is almost as big as Jupiter, and like Jupiter is made mainly of gas. It is twice as far from the Sun as Jupiter. Its most interesting features are its rings. Uranus, Neptune and Jupiter also have rings. They are made of ice and rock particles which never condensed to form moons.

Three other planets lie beyond Saturn: Uranus, Neptune and Pluto. From them the Sun would appear no bigger than a bright star.

▼ **This picture shows the Sun and planets** to the same scale. The Sun is huge compared with its planets, but is only an average-sized star. The Sun is 1,400,000km (865,000 miles) wide. Jupiter which is the largest planet is 1,430,000km (88,700 miles) wide, while Mercury, the smallest, is only about 4,800km (3000 miles) wide.

Besides the planets and their moons, the Solar System contains thousands of asteroids and comets. The asteroids are small and rocky. The Voyager space probes flew through the asteroids in 1978 and took excellent pictures of all four giant planets.

Comets are made of dust, ice and frozen gases. The gases are vaporized by the Sun's rays when a comet approaches the Sun. The gases start to glow, and extend to form a tail. The tail can be millions of miles long but only a few comets are bright enough to be seen from Earth without a telescope.

▼ **The Sun** (arrowed) compared with a section of the red-giant star Aldebaran, which is over 48 million kilometres (30 million miles) across.

Mars has two dwarf moons – Phobos and Deimos. They are both less than 32km (20 miles) across.

Jupiter has 16 moons. The 16th was only discovered in 1980.

MERCURY
Moon
VENUS
EARTH
MARS
ASTEROID BELT
JUPITER

◀ **Most of the planets go round the Sun** in near-circular orbits. The exception is Pluto (arrowed) which has an oval orbit. In 1979 Pluto passed inside the orbit of Neptune. They will not collide, but for over 20 years, Neptune will be the outermost planet.

Moons and asteroids

Seven of the nine planets in the Solar System have satellites (moons). Most of these moons are much smaller than the planets they circle. However Pluto and its moon, Charon, are almost the same size, and the Earth is only four times as wide as its moon. Four planets have several moons: Jupiter 16, Saturn 17, Uranus 15 and Neptune 8. Jupiter's largest moon, Ganymede, is bigger than Mercury, or almost half as wide as Earth.

Between Mars and Jupiter lies the Asteroid Belt. This is made up of thousands of objects too small to be called planets. They could be what was left after the planets formed, or the remains of a tenth planet. Ceres, the biggest asteroid, is 1,000km (620 miles) across.

Even if all the mysteries of the Solar System were solved, we would still only be on the threshold of the age of space exploration. Scientists believe that millions of other stars may have families of planets around them awaiting discovery.

▼ **Giant explosions on the face of the Sun** are called prominences. They are made of glowing gas and can be huge. A prominence seen in June, 1946 rose over 200,000 miles above the surface of the Sun. On the same scale as the drawing, this prominence would extend more than two inches over the top of the page. Compare the size of this with the tiny Earth shown on the left.

Saturn has 17 moons. Titan, the largest, has a thickish atmosphere of nitrogen. Its surface is covered with frozen gases.

Uranus has 15 moons. They are all much smaller than our own Moon.

Neptune has eight moons. The largest is about 4,800km (3000 miles) wide.

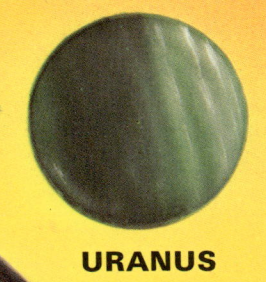

PLUTO

Pluto has one moon.

SATURN

URANUS

NEPTUNE

COMETS

Astronomers now think that a huge "halo" of comets lies outside the orbit of Pluto.

INTO INFINITY

Distances in space are huge and writing about them with ordinary measurements involves dozens of noughts. So another measurement is used – the light-year.

A light-year is equal to 9,500,000 million kilometres (5,880,000 million miles). This is the distance that light travels in one year. The speed of light is 300,000km (186,281 miles) a second.

The distances in the Universe are so vast that it would take more than a million years to travel one light-year at a speed of 1,000kph (600mph).

A star called the Sun

Light takes about eight minutes to reach the Earth from the Sun. The Sun is a star. It is only one among the millions of stars that can be seen from Earth. These are all part of our Galaxy. There are millions of other stars in the Galaxy, too, that we can't see.

The name 'galaxy' comes from the Greek word for milk. It was given first to the huge cluster of stars that we can often see on a fine night, so close together that they look like a white stream – the Milky Way. Then galaxy came to mean the whole system of stars, seen and unseen, of which our Sun is one. Later, other clusters of stars were discovered, and they were called galaxies too.

Neighbour stars

The star nearest to our Sun is 4.2 light-years away. It is in the constellation of Centaurus, and is called Proxima Centauri. It has two companion stars. The brightest is Alpha Centauri. This group of stars is 7,000 times farther from the Sun than Pluto, the farthest away of the Sun's planets.

The brightest star in the sky is called Sirius – the Dog Star. It is 8.7 light-years away, or more than twice as far away as Alpha Centauri.

The ten or so nearest stars are so far away that their light takes several years to reach us. But the stars at the other end of the Galaxy are 100,000 light-years away.

Not all the stars in the Galaxy are like our Sun. Some are much hotter, some are colder. The difference in their temperatures can be seen from their colours. As with a flame, the hotter ones look blue and white. The cooler ones look red.

The stars all vary in size, too. There is a very large red star in the constellation of Orion. It is called Betelgeuse. It is 250 times bigger than the Sun, but is only half as hot.

Double star systems

Some stars are really multiple stars. This means that two stars are orbiting round each other, or even round a third star. There are a lot of double star systems.

Our Galaxy contains millions of stars – more than 100,000 million. But it is only one galaxy among 1,000 million others. Our nearest galaxies are the Magellanic Clouds. They are small, irregular galaxies and can be seen in the southern hemisphere. Another galaxy which you can just see with the naked eye is in the constellation of Andromeda. It is spiral-shaped like our own.

Distant galaxies

The biggest telescopes can see galaxies which are over 10 thousand million light years away. The Earth was not even formed when the light of these galaxies began its journey through space.

The Universe is expanding, rather like a balloon being blown up. Some galaxies are moving away from ours at over half the speed of light. We cannot see beyond them. They are not even at the edge of the Universe. They are only at the edge of the part of it that we can see.

Life and death of the Sun

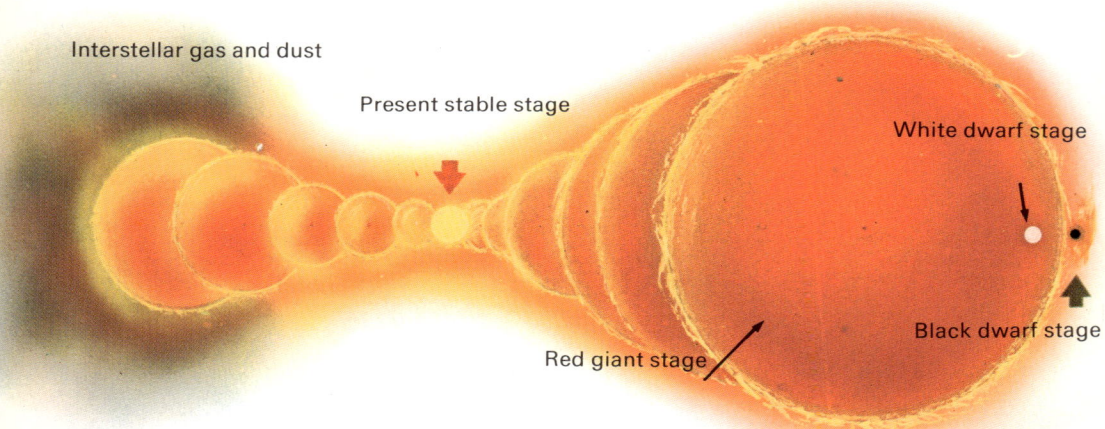

Interstellar gas and dust

Present stable stage

White dwarf stage

Black dwarf stage

Red giant stage

▲ **The Sun** probably began life as a huge cloud of gas and dust. This contracted, grew hotter and began to spin. It entered its present stable stage when it became hot and compact enough for nuclear reactions to begin. It will eventually expand again, as the nuclear fuel is used up, and then collapse, ending up as a cinder-like black dwarf.

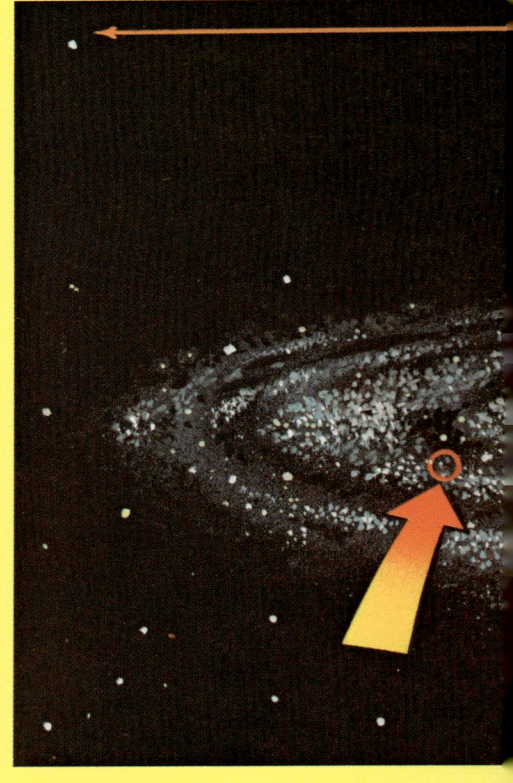

Man's small world

The Earth is one of the smaller planets of the Sun. Seen from halfway to the Moon, it looks like a hazy blue ball. The blue tint is caused by the atmosphere, a layer of air that, on the scale of the picture, is about as thick as a page of this book. A covering of cloud obscures the surface, though the shape of continents can be glimpsed from time to time beneath it. A visitor from space with eyesight equivalent to man's would have to come to within about 240km (150 miles) to find any signs of human life.

◀ **Earth lies** 150 million kilometres (93 million miles), or eight light-minutes, from the Sun. This means that we see the Sun as it was eight minutes ago.

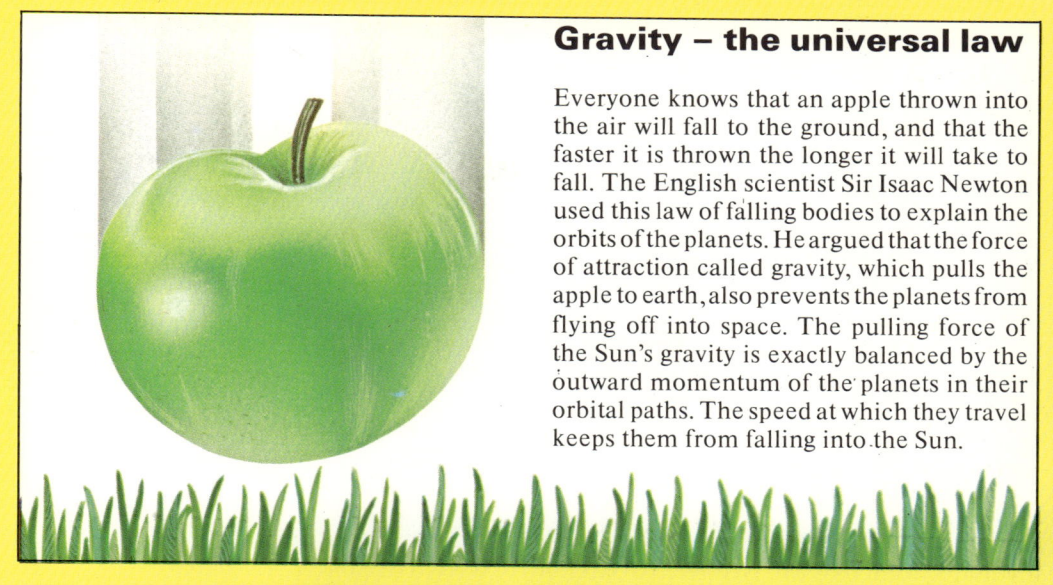

Gravity – the universal law

Everyone knows that an apple thrown into the air will fall to the ground, and that the faster it is thrown the longer it will take to fall. The English scientist Sir Isaac Newton used this law of falling bodies to explain the orbits of the planets. He argued that the force of attraction called gravity, which pulls the apple to earth, also prevents the planets from flying off into space. The pulling force of the Sun's gravity is exactly balanced by the outward momentum of the planets in their orbital paths. The speed at which they travel keeps them from falling into the Sun.

100,000 light-years

Lost in the Milky Way...

Our Sun is one of more than 100,000 million stars in the Milky Way Galaxy. On a scale map of the Galaxy on which the Earth was 2.5cm (1in) from the Sun, the nearest star would lie 6.4km (4 miles) away.

The illustration above shows what the Milky Way would look like if seen from the side, while the one on the left shows it from above. The arrowed circles show where our Solar System lies, though on this scale it would be too small to see even through a microscope.

The whole Galaxy is spinning, like a giant Catherine-wheel. It revolves in one cosmic year – about 225 million of our years. There is evidence that some other stars in the Milky Way may have planets as the Sun has, though no telescope is powerful enough for men to see them.

Elliptical galaxy

Barred galaxy

Irregular galaxy

◀ **The Milky way itself** is only a tiny part of the Universe. This illustration shows other galaxies in the cluster to which the Milky Way (left) belongs. They take various shapes, and some have no recognizable form at all.

Even neighbour galaxies like these are so far away that their light takes millions of years to reach us. Man had not evolved when it started its journey.

PIONEERS WHO SHOWED THE WAY TO THE STARS

Before the invention of the space rocket, space had to be explored from the ground, through telescopes. This is still the chief way of learning about the Universe.

The telescope was invented in the early 1600s in Holland. But the first man to use it for looking at the stars was an Italian, Galileo. He improved the telescope and made many discoveries, including the four large moons of Jupiter.

New light on the stars

But Galileo's telescope was still very simple. In the 1700s better ones were invented. Men like the British astronomer Herschel were able to see millions of stars for the first time. The planets Uranus and Neptune were discovered, as well as the moons around Saturn.

In the 1800s telescopes became so much better that men at last began to understand the enormous size of the Universe.

Modern telescopes are very big indeed. They are housed in large observatories and have motors to move them. The largest telescope in the world is in the Soviet Union. It is 5.6m (236in) in diameter.

The discovery of Pluto

Much more was learnt about the stars when photographs could be taken through telescopes. The ninth planet, Pluto, was discovered in this way in 1930. Scientists had worked out that there must be another planet somewhere beyond Neptune, and Pluto was finally found by comparing photographs of the same section of the night sky on different days.

Scientists also found that they could learn what stars were made of by analyzing the light that came from them. Each element, such as hydrogen and oxygen, makes a different pattern of colours in an instrument called a spectroscope.

In the 1930s the radio telescope was invented. Stars, galaxies and gas clouds give out radio waves as well as light. Radio telescopes can pick up these signals. They reveal invisible gas clouds and carry information about spinning stars, exploding stars, and black holes.

The first space rockets

At about the same time as the radio telescope was invented, an American, Robert H. Goddard, was experimenting with rocket propulsion.

During the Second World War scientists in Germany developed the first real space rocket, called the V2. But it was a weapon of war, used for bombarding London.

When peace came in 1945 both America and Russia went on developing these

Heroes of astronomy and their primitive telescopes

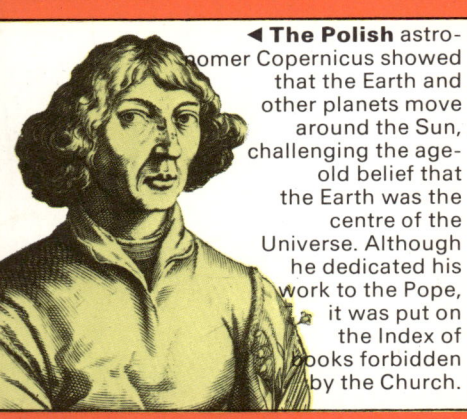

◀ **The Polish** astronomer Copernicus showed that the Earth and other planets move around the Sun, challenging the age-old belief that the Earth was the centre of the Universe. Although he dedicated his work to the Pope, it was put on the Index of books forbidden by the Church.

◀ **A Dane,** Tycho Brahe (1546-1601), was the greatest astronomical observer of the pre-telescope age, even though he wrongly believed that the Sun moved around the Earth. His pupil Johannes Kepler used his records to discover that the planets move in elliptical (oval) orbits.

◀ **Italy's** Galileo (1564-1642) was the first great astronomer to use the newly-invented telescope. His support of Copernicus's theory upset Church authorities, who forced him to renounce his views publicly, under threat of torture.

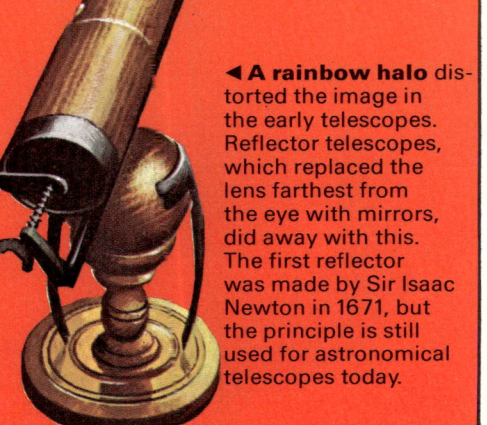

◀ **From 1609,** Galileo pioneered telescope astronomy with simple instruments like the two shown mounted for exhibition here. The longer one magnified objects about 20 times – enough for Galileo to discover the four largest moons of Jupiter and draw the first detailed map of the Moon.

◀ **A rainbow halo** distorted the image in the early telescopes. Reflector telescopes, which replaced the lens farthest from the eye with mirrors, did away with this. The first reflector was made by Sir Isaac Newton in 1671, but the principle is still used for astronomical telescopes today.

Giant tool for a giant Universe – the radio telescope at Arecibo, Puerto Rico

Helicopter landing pad

rockets, not only as weapons but for scientific research too. A German scientist who had worked on the wartime rockets was now helping the Americans. His name was Wernher von Braun. He wanted to use rockets to send a man into space.

The Russians were the first to send up an artificial satellite to orbit the Earth. It was called Sputnik 1, and it was launched in October, 1957. The rocket used was the same as that used for carrying nuclear missiles.

The Space Race begins

The Americans sent up their first satellite only four months later. It was called Explorer 1. This began the Space Race, and for years the Americans and the Russians competed with each other in exploring space. Now they have agreed to help each other in some projects.

The first man in space was a Russian, Yuri Gagarin. He orbited the Earth in a Vostok spacecraft on April 12, 1961. This was only three and a half years after the first satellite had been put into space.

The Russians were also the first to land a robot explorer on the Moon. This was Luna 9, in 1966. It sent back TV pictures of the Moon to the Earth.

Man walks on the Moon

In 1969 came the greatest achievement of all. The Americans Neil Armstrong and Edwin Aldrin became the first men to walk on the Moon. The date was July 20.

Six expeditions were made to the Moon. Moon rock was brought back for scientists to examine. Many experiments were set up on the surface.

Russia and America, as well as a few other countries, have launched thousands of satellites between them. Robot spacecraft have been sent to photograph other planets in the Solar System. Other craft have landed on Mars and Venus.

Space scientists choose the time and path of these space probes very carefully. The same spacecraft can be used to send back information from more than one planet as it flies by. The pull of a planet's gravity can be used to make the spacecraft go faster than it does when it is launched.

The American spacecraft Pioneer 10 and 11 were the first to visit the outer planets beyond the asteroids. Launched in 1972 and 1973, they both flew past Jupiter and Pioneer 11 flew past Saturn in 1979. Pioneer 10 became the first spacecraft to cross Pluto's orbit and leave the solar system in 1987, followed by Pioneer 11. They carry plaques that explain in diagrams where they were launched.

Today's astronomers

The early explorers of space were astronomers. They worked on their own and took years to publish their results. Today the exploration is done with radio telescopes, satellites and space probes as well as with large optical telescopes. Thousands of people all over the world are working on it. A great deal of money is spent. As a result something new is discovered almost every day.

Radio waves moving through space are intercepted by the reflector.

A bowl 300m (1,000ft) wide, covered with aluminium sheets, bounces the rays up to the aerial.

The signals are carried down a feed line from the aerial to the operations building.

How the Arecibo 'ear' works

1 Signals received by the suspended aerial are fed to a detector and amplified to make the signals stronger.

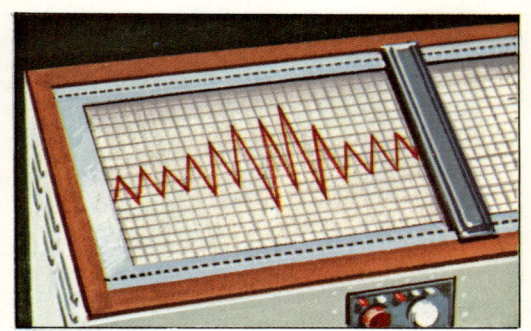

2 A recorder linked to the detector traces the waves' intensity on graph paper. Results can be rapidly analyzed by computer.

3 Incoming signals are simultaneously recorded on tape for storage. Patterns of sound can be checked by playback.

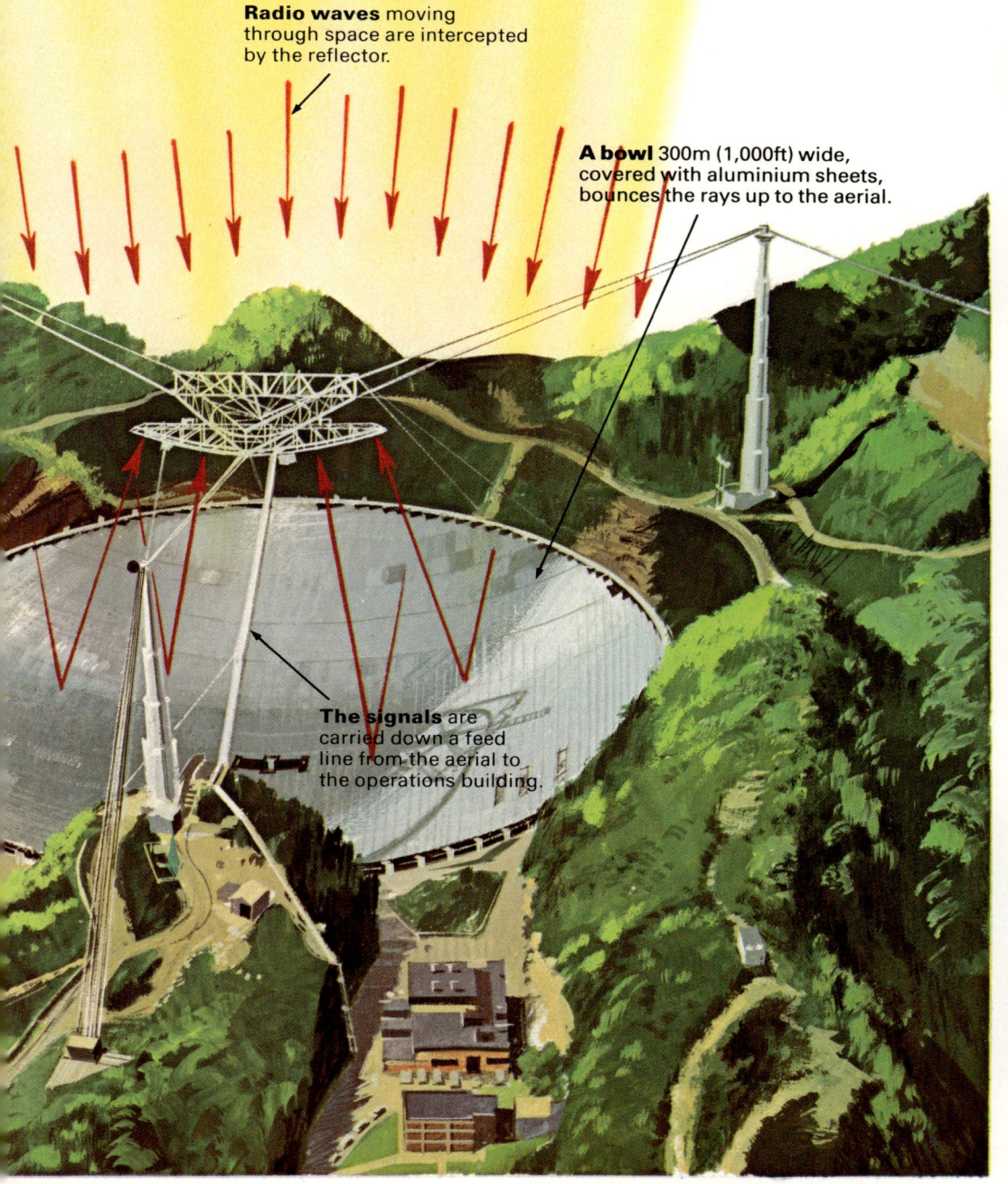

ROBOT EXPLORERS

◀ **Luna 1** was the first Russian Moon probe. In 1959, it passed within 5,000km (3,100 miles) of the Moon, and continued into orbit around the Sun.

Solar panels

▶ **Luna 16** left the Moon in 1970, after extracting rock and soil samples with the help of a drill.

◀ **Lunar Orbiters** helped NASA scientists select landing sites for the Apollo astronauts by sending photos of the Moon's surface from orbit.

Radio signals

Camera viewing angle

◀ **Ranger 7** was sent to photograph the Moon in 1964, to provide information on landing conditions for future probes. It sent back more than 4,000 close-up photographs before crashing into the Sea of Clouds.

▼ **Lunokhod 1**, launched by the Russians in 1970, was the first mobile explorer. It went down a ramp from its landing craft. Under remote control from Earth, it then travelled more than 9.5km (6 miles) on the Moon, taking photographs and studying soil samples.

▼ **Pioneer 10** flew within 130,000km (81,000 miles) of Jupiter in 1973, photographing it five times more clearly than is possible from Earth. It has now left the solar system.

Sun's rays

▼ **Russia's Luna 9** made the first controlled landing on the Moon in 1966. The lander ejected an egg-shaped capsule that rolled away from the craft. It then opened up, exposing four aerials and a small TV camera.

Solar cells provide power

▲ **Unmanned craft** have been the pioneers of space discovery since Sputnik 1. They have explored all the planets except Pluto.

The best way for man to explore space is to go there himself. But this costs a lot of money. A man has to take all his air and food with him. The spacecraft has to be large enough to hold him and his fellow-astronauts. A great deal of effort is spent in bringing the spacecraft and the astronauts back to Earth. It is easier and much cheaper to use machines.

Robot explorers, as these machines are called, are still expensive. But they can be made smaller than manned spacecraft. The rocket that launches them does not have to be nearly as powerful.

News from the planets

Robot explorers can send back information which helps men to prepare their own expeditions to the planets. They have discovered new moons and studied the surfaces and atmospheres of almost all the planets.

A robot explorer can fly past a planet, taking pictures as it passes, or it can orbit a planet and take a series of pictures or it can land on the planet itself.

Fly-by space probes

Several spacecraft have made fly-by trips. Pioneers 10 and 11 passed Jupiter and 11 went on to pass Saturn. Mariner 9 went into orbit around Mars, and Mariner 10 flew past Mercury and Venus.

The gravity of the planets can be used to help pull spacecraft on their way. This saves fuel and was used for Voyagers 1 and 2 which flew by Jupiter and Saturn. Voyager 2 also went on to visit Uranus in 1986 and Neptune in 1989.

An orbiting spacecraft can send back many hundreds of pictures before its batteries run out or it crashes into the planet. Maps can be made of the planet's surface. The Mariner spacecraft took a lot of pictures of Mars. These showed for the first time that Mars has craters, like the Moon, as well as the biggest volcano in the Solar System – Olympus Mons.

The Venus landing

In 1975 the Russians sent two Venera spacecraft to the planet Venus. They only survived for an hour. But they sent back photographs and information about the planet's very high temperature and dense poisonous atmosphere. The pictures showed a surface covered in rocks.

Spacecraft like Venera which are heading for a planet eject a capsule from the mothercraft for landing. A heatshield pro-

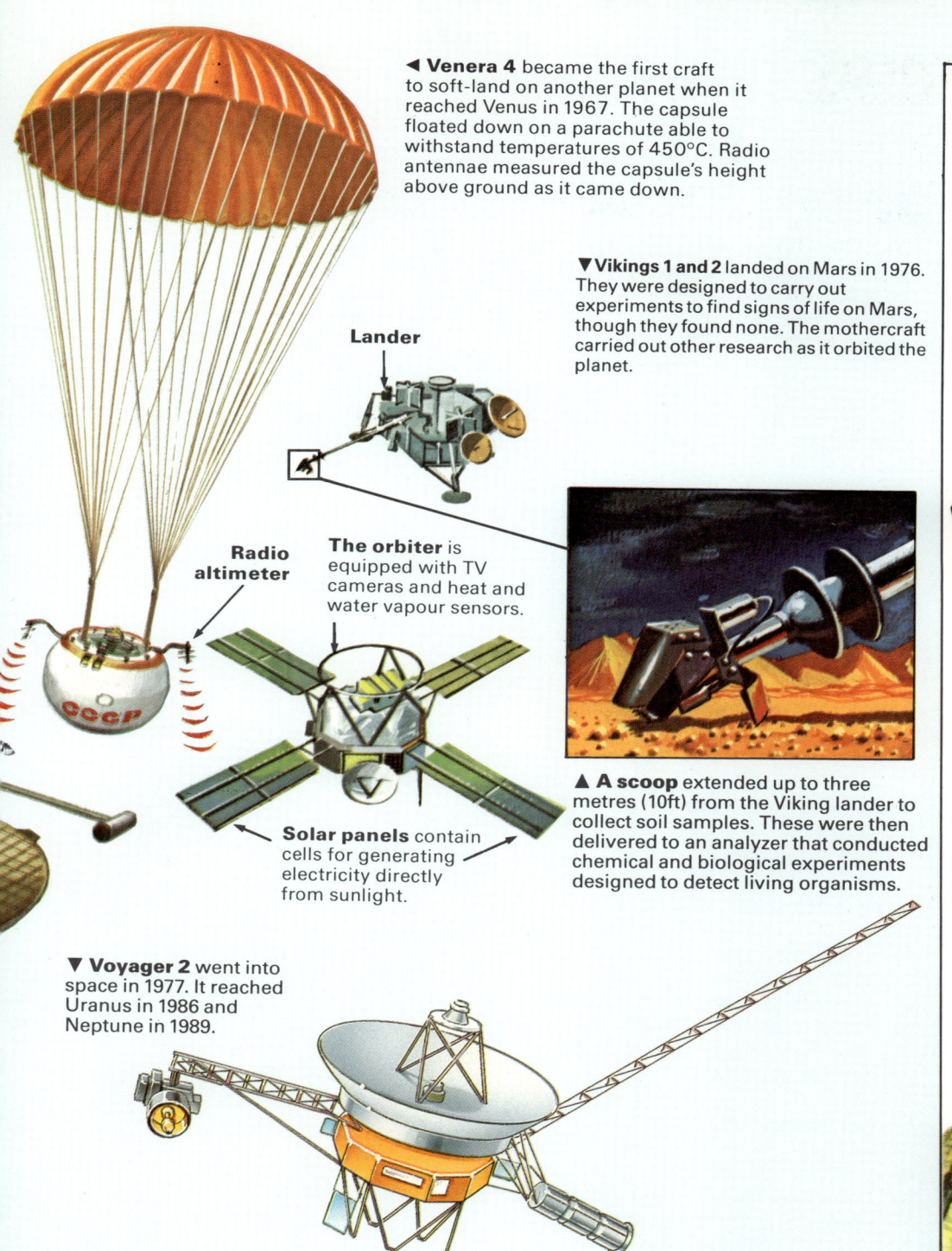

◀ **Venera 4** became the first craft to soft-land on another planet when it reached Venus in 1967. The capsule floated down on a parachute able to withstand temperatures of 450°C. Radio antennae measured the capsule's height above ground as it came down.

▼ **Vikings 1 and 2** landed on Mars in 1976. They were designed to carry out experiments to find signs of life on Mars, though they found none. The mothercraft carried out other research as it orbited the planet.

Lander

Radio altimeter

The orbiter is equipped with TV cameras and heat and water vapour sensors.

Solar panels contain cells for generating electricity directly from sunlight.

▲ **A scoop** extended up to three metres (10ft) from the Viking lander to collect soil samples. These were then delivered to an analyzer that conducted chemical and biological experiments designed to detect living organisms.

▼ **Voyager 2** went into space in 1977. It reached Uranus in 1986 and Neptune in 1989.

Animal astronauts

Robot explorers told scientists a lot, but they could not tell them what would happen to living bodies when they left Earth's atmosphere. To find out more about this, animals – especially dogs and monkeys – were sent on experimental flights.

▲ **A dog called Laika** was the first living creature to travel in space. She orbited the Earth in Sputnik 2, which was launched in the early days of the Space Age in 1957. Sadly, Laika died in orbit when the satellite's air supply ran out.

▼ **Ham,** a 62kg (137lb) chimpanzee, survived a series of mishaps on an American test flight in 1961. The rocket flew higher than intended, and a pressure bulkhead was punctured as it returned to Earth, but Ham was recovered unhurt.

tects the capsule as it passes through the atmosphere. Then parachutes slow down its descent and the instruments start to radio information back to Earth.

Coasting through space

The spacecraft carrying the capsule to the planet does not need to carry much fuel. The speed of the craft is provided by the launch. The rocket 'coasts' to its destination. Small rockets are used to correct the course during the flight.

Most robot spacecraft use power from the Sun. Solar panels give energy to the crafts' batteries. The batteries supply power for the other equipment.

Robot explorers were sent to the Moon before the first manned landing. Their main task was to help scientists to select a landing site. Scientists feared that on the Moon's surface there might be a layer of dust deep enough to swallow a spacecraft. Surveyor 3 dug a small trench while scientists watched on TV. This showed that it was safe to try a landing.

The Russians have so far used only robot spacecraft to explore the Moon. One of these, Lunokhod, moved around on the Moon's surface on wheels, operated by remote control from Earth, and sent back TV pictures. Another type of craft landed and brought back rock samples.

Looking for life on Mars

Two American Viking spacecraft were launched in 1975 and landed on Mars in 1976. The landing sites were chosen from the pictures sent back by Mariner 9. Their aim was to search for signs of life on the planet.

Scientists had to build a very small device which could make experiments normally only done in a laboratory. When Viking landed, it drove out a mechanical scoop into the Martian soil. The scoop pulled back soil into the spacecraft and analysed it for things which were necessary for life, like proteins. Disappointingly there was no sign of life at all.

The Viking landers sent back TV pictures in colour. They showed the surface of Mars is covered in red rocks and dust. The red colour comes from rust. The sky is pink because of dust in the air.

The spacecraft had been sterilized so as not to take germs or viruses to Mars. This means, too, that if life was found the scientists would know it was not something carried from Earth.

Robot explorers are preparing the way to the planets. Sometime in the future, men will follow.

SURVIVING IN SPACE

Spaceship Earth's blanket of air

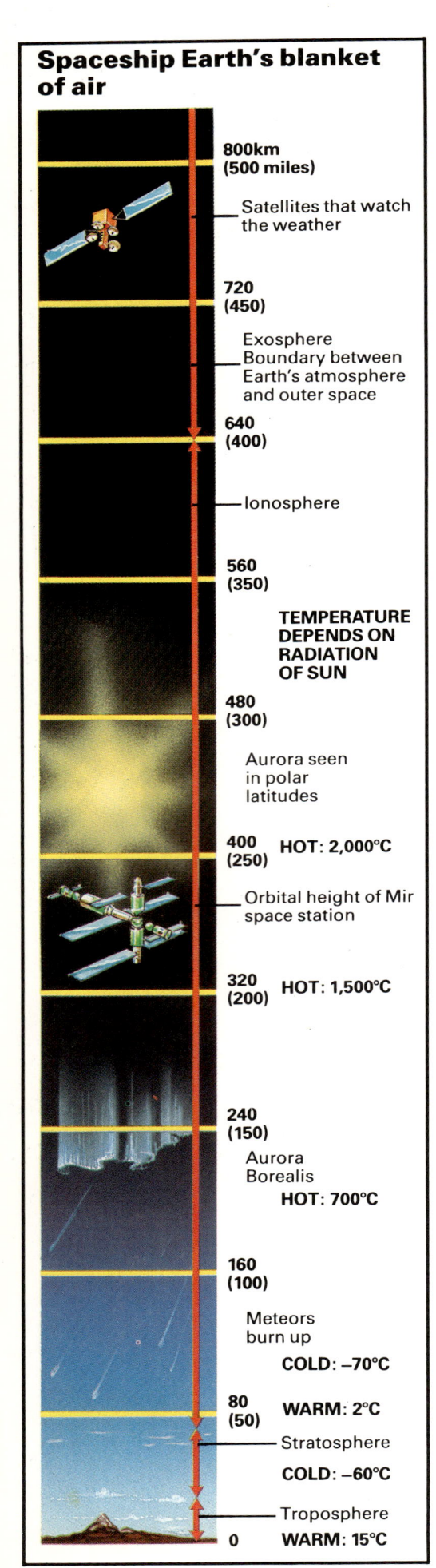

800km (500 miles) — Satellites that watch the weather
720 (450)
Exosphere Boundary between Earth's atmosphere and outer space
640 (400)
Ionosphere
560 (350)
TEMPERATURE DEPENDS ON RADIATION OF SUN
480 (300)
Aurora seen in polar latitudes
400 (250) HOT: 2,000°C
Orbital height of Mir space station
320 (200) HOT: 1,500°C
240 (150) Aurora Borealis HOT: 700°C
160 (100) Meteors burn up COLD: −70°C
80 (50) WARM: 2°C
Stratosphere
COLD: −60°C
Troposphere
0 WARM: 15°C

Humans cannot live in space unless they wear special clothing. This is needed to keep the body under pressure and to provide oxygen to breathe. It also keeps the body at the right temperature and protects against radiation and speeding space dust called micrometeoroids.

On the Earth the body is kept under constant pressure by the atmosphere pressing down on it. In space there is no atmosphere and so no pressure. Without a space suit to maintain this pressure the blood would boil, killing the astronaut.

The cabin of a spacecraft is filled with air to keep the pressure high enough for the astronauts to breathe normally and wear ordinary clothing.

Dressing for space travel

When astronauts are on board a shuttle or space station orbiting the Earth they wear ordinary clothing or overalls with lots of pockets for pens, notepads and tools which would float about if not held down. If they want to stay in one place they can wear shoes with suction cups that stick to the floor.

During launch and when returning to Earth, astronauts wear pressure suits and helmets for added safety.

Near the end of a long stay in space, Russian cosmonauts wear special trousers which help pull their blood down towards the lower half of the body as gravity does on Earth. In space, where there is no gravity, their blood tends to rise to the upper parts of the body.

Out in space

When an astronaut leaves his spacecraft or space station to work out in space, he wears a space suit. Underneath it he wears a cooling suit with tubes containing water. These keep him cool even in the hot sunlight in space. The space suit itself has many layers to maintain the pressure and insulate him from the extreme heat and cold of space. A strong outer layer protects from tearing and micrometeoroids.

The American suit is made in two halves. The trousers, with boots attached, are put on first. Then the astronaut slides into the rigid upper half which is mounted on the wall. The two halves snap together at the waist and then gloves and helmet are snapped on.

The Russian space suits are all in one piece. They get into it by climbing through a door at the back. It has flexible joints at the shoulder, elbow, hip and knee for movement. Space suits are very bulky and heavy on Earth but in space, with no gravity, they weigh almost nothing.

Helmet and backpack

The helmet has a visor to protect the astronaut's eyes from the Sun and from micrometeoroids. Under the helmet there

---

▼ **Space suits** are man-shaped containers replacing Earth's atmosphere in space. Their main purposes are to provide oxygen, and the pressure and temperature conditions men need to live in. They also remove body wastes like urine, excess sweat and carbon dioxide breathed out by the wearer.

Suits vary in details depending on the job they are made for. On the Moon astronauts wore coveralls over their pressure suits to protect them from the Sun's heat. Otherwise Moon suits were similar to those used for space walks.

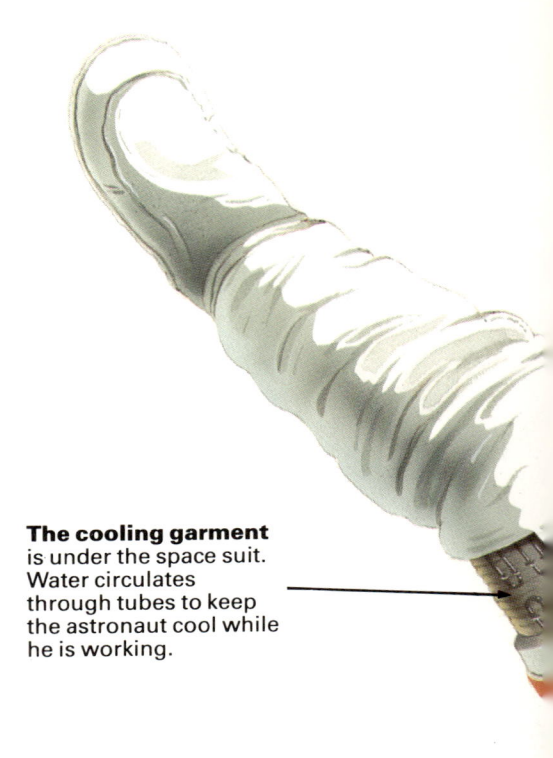

The cooling garment is under the space suit. Water circulates through tubes to keep the astronaut cool while he is working.

The control panel monitors all of the suit's functions such as the amount of oxygen and the suit pressure. It also controls communications with the shuttle and ground control.

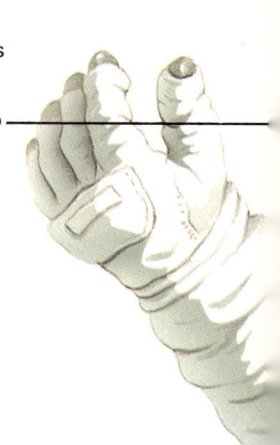

A backpack made of glass fibre contains the life support system that makes activity outside the spacecraft possible. It supplies oxygen, and cleans returned air of carbon dioxide. It pumps water through the piped cooling system and provides power for radio communication. The astronaut can adjust it by means of the control pack on his chest.

The shoes are attached to the trousers, which snap onto the torso at the waist.

Several layers of material lie beneath the suit's white nylon cover. An underlay of meshed nylon gives the suit strength. Airtight rubber keeps the pressure maintained in the suit from escaping.

Gloves are insulated to protect the hands from extreme heat or cold. Soft rubber finger tips help the astronaut feel things.

Lights help the astronaut see to work.

The helmet locks into a pressure-tight ring attachment on the suit. The visor is tinted to cut down the sun's glare, and is strong enough for micrometeoroids to bounce off it.

The TV camera sends pictures to the shuttle and ground control.

is a cap with headphones and a microphone for talking to other astronauts.

On his back the astronaut wears a backpack called a portable life support system. This carries oxygen to breathe and to supply pressure, water for cooling and a battery for power. It circulates the water and oxygen through the suit and removes the carbon dioxide breathed out by the astronaut. It has enough supplies for up to seven hours outside the spacecraft.

All the controls are mounted on a panel on the astronaut's chest where he can see them. A warning signal shows when his oxygen supply is getting low.

Living in space

Cosmonauts have now lived in the Mir space station for just over a year. Living in space even for short stays affects the human body, though it soon returns to normal back on Earth. Without gravity always pulling downwards astronauts become a few centimetres taller. Their faces get a little puffy and their muscles can get weak, so it is very important to exercise regularly. They use an exercise bicycle or treadmill to run on. Many astronauts suffer from space sickness, just like travel sickness, for the first few days in space.

Diseases in space

When men first went to the Moon it was thought they might bring back germs that could cause diseases harmful to humans. When they returned they were kept away from other people for three weeks. However all the tests showed that there was no life of any kind on the Moon and no disease to catch.

Scientists also thought there might be life on Mars. The Viking spacecraft that landed there carried experiments to test for signs of life. Although some of the results were surprising, they did not prove that there was any life.

Getting around in space

Astronauts out in space are usually tethered to their spacecraft by cable to stop them floating off. If they want to go further away from the spacecraft, they have to wear a Manned Manoeuvring Unit (MMU) attached to their back pack. The American one has 24 small jets powered by nitrogen gas. They allow the astronaut to move and turn in any direction. It looks rather like an armchair, with the controls on the end of the arms.

Into orbit with the shuttle

1 Space shuttles went into operation in 1981. They are built by the Americans. This picture shows how they are launched.

2 The two booster rockets separate from the shuttle by firing small sideways thrust rockets. The boosters parachute into the sea.

3 The empty fuel tank is jettisoned as the shuttle moves into orbit. There is no prospect of salvaging this – unlike the boosters.

SPACE SHUTTLES AND SPACE CITIES

The spacecraft that took the American astronauts to the Moon could only be used once. Each cost 150,000 million dollars. Now, spacecraft are being built that can be used several times. This should make space travel cheaper and allow more people to go into space.

The spacecraft that can take them is called a space shuttle. It will be able to travel to and from orbiting space stations.

Boosters and orbiters

The American space shuttle is almost all re-usable. It consists of an orbiter which looks rather like an aeroplane, a huge fuel tank and two booster rockets.

It takes off vertically like a rocket, using the orbiter's engines and the boosters. These seperate at a height of about 45km (28 miles) and parachute down into the sea to be used again. The fuel tank which feeds the orbiter's main engines is not used again. It burns up in the atmosphere.

The orbiter circles the Earth and will visit future space stations. When it returns to Earth it lands on a runway, without engines, like a huge glider. The orbiter and booster rockets are then prepared for another flight.

The shuttle first flew in space in 1981. Since then it has launched satellites into space and carried many experiments. It can take a complete laboratory called Spacelab into space, and in 1990 it put the giant Space Telescope into orbit. Shuttles will also ferry the parts to build a large space station in orbit, and will carry passengers and supplies up to the completed station.

Space laboratories like Spacelab and the early space station, Skylab, give scientists more information about the Sun and distant universe. In space, the Earth's atmosphere does not get in the way. The Space Telescope will see further and clearer than telescopes on Earth.

Aboard space stations

Skylab was a large American space station launched in 1973. It carried special telescopes to study the Sun. Three different teams of astronauts worked aboard Skylab in 1973-4.

Scientists on the shuttles and the Mir space station take photographs of Earth and study its problems. Satellites also provide valuable information about the weather and can analyze soil conditions and detect crop diseases.

In the future engineers will be able to study the best ways of building and assembling spaceships in orbit. Because they will be free of Earth's gravity, the metals they use will be weightless.

There will be several space stations orbiting the Earth. Space 'tugs' will be used outside the space stations. Mechanical arms will be used to dock the shuttles, unload cargo and do repair work.

Ferries to the Moon

Once the space stations have been established it will be easier to travel to and from the Moon. A spacecraft will make regular trips between space stations orbiting the Earth and others orbiting the Moon.

Spacecraft of the future may be powered by nuclear engines. These engines would be smaller and more powerful than the present rocket engines

Reducing waste

When a large satellite or spacecraft is put into orbit round the Earth, part of the launching rocket sometimes stays in orbit too. There are a lot of these rocket stages in space now. At the moment they are no use to anyone. But in the future there will be no need to waste them. They could be used to build extra parts of the space stations.

Space stations of the more distant future will be bigger. Some of them may be made to spin to create a force in part of the space station that will be something like Earth's gravity. But it is its freedom from Earth's gravity that will make the space station especially useful.

Space stations are the essential stepping-stones to the other planets. Together with the space shuttle they will make spaceflight as normal in the next century as flying the Atlantic is today.

Scientists in orbit

Mir space station

Mir, a Russian space station now in orbit around the Earth, was launched in 1986. It has been built up in space, by adding three extra modules with telescopes for studying space and equipment for growing large crystals used to make computers.

Mir has a crew of two cosmonauts, with visiting crews of two or three people for short stays. Air, water, food and fuel are brought up from Earth.

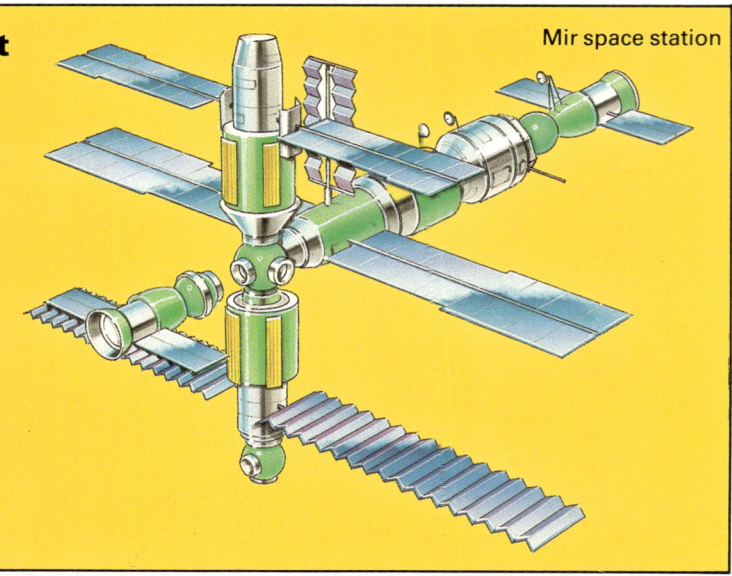

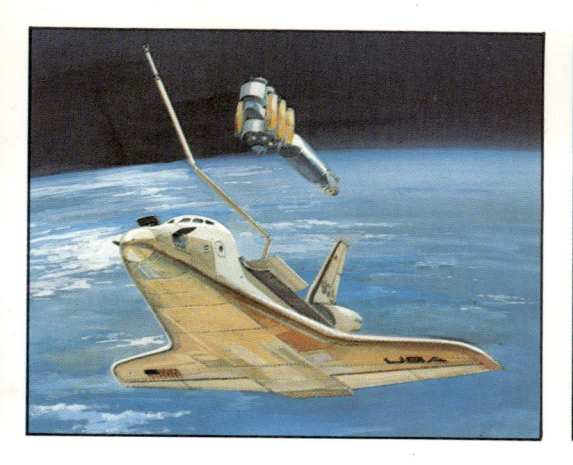

4 The cargo bay doors open, and the shuttle places its payload, a weather satellite, in orbit with a jointed handling arm.

5 Mission accomplished, the shuttle fires its retro rockets to set it on course back to Earth. It glides back into the atmosphere.

6 The shuttle lands like a huge glider on the runway at Kennedy Space Centre – ready to be re-used at least 100 times.

Cities in the sky

One answer to overcrowding on Earth may be to send people to live in space. An American professor called Gerard O'Neill has worked out designs for living-cylinders miles long that could be put into orbit between the Earth and the Moon. The cylinders would spin to create Earth-like gravity conditions. Sunlight reflected into the craft through mirrors would create a perfect climate for thousands of people living in 'valleys' with soil and trees.

1. **Mirrors** can be opened to create 'days' and closed for 'nights'.
2. **Windows** let sunlight into cylinder.
3. **Valleys** lie opposite each solar. They have artificial mountains, lakes and rivers as well as houses and shops. Clouds form naturally above them.
4. **Docking bays** for visiting spacecraft.
5. **Power-station mirror** reflects the Sun's rays onto boilers in generator.
6. **Generator** creates electricity for all the colonists' power needs.
7. **Ring of small cylinders** to house polluting activities like industry.
8. **Twin cities** are joined by cables to prevent 'wobble' caused by rotation.

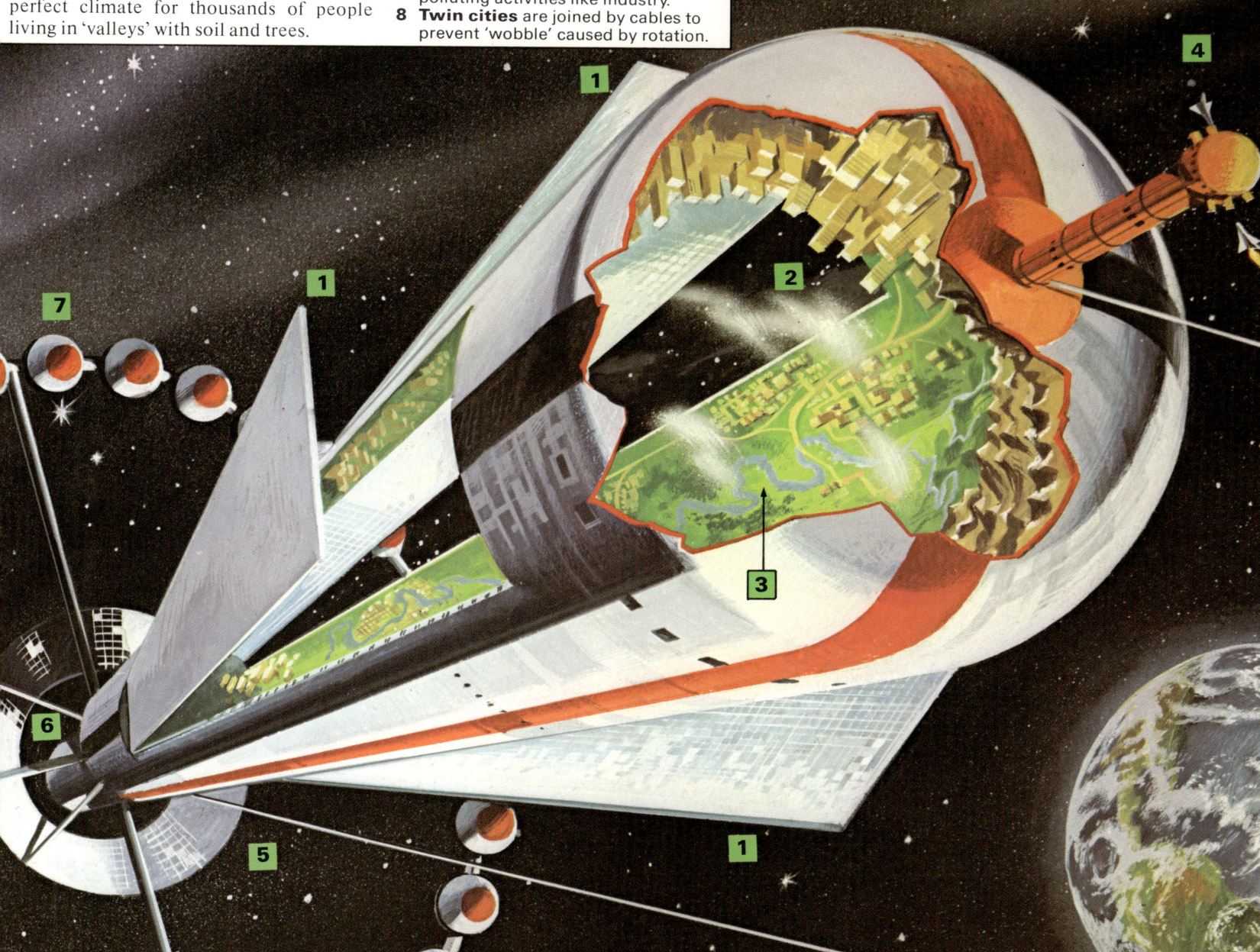

TIMECHART

c. 2800 B.C.	Babylonian astronomers give names to many constellations
c. 1100 B.C.	Chinese astronomers active. Comets observed.
c. 260 B.C.	The Greek astronomer Aristarchus of Samos states that the Earth goes round the Sun, but few people believe his theories.
c. 130 B.C.	Hipparchus of Alexandria catalogues 1080 stars, dividing them into magnitudes of brightness for the first time.
c. 140 A.D.	Ptolemy of Alexandria's book 'Almagest' sums up everything then known about the Universe. It was the basis of astronomical studies for the next 1200 years.
700-c.1450	Arab astronomers improve the star catalogues and observations of the Greeks, and make great advances in practical astronomy.
1543	Copernicus publishes his theory of the Universe, showing that the Earth goes round the Sun.
1609	Kepler publishes a book about Mars. He shows that the planets move round the Sun in elliptical orbits.
1610	Galileo publishes the first results of his observations with the telescope, invented two years earlier by Lippershey in Holland.
1659	The Dutch astronomer Huygens sees Saturn's rings.
1668	Sir Isaac Newton constructs the first reflecting telescope.
1718	Halley discovers that the stars move in space.
1930	Pluto, the last of the Sun's planets, discovered.
1936	Reber builds the first radio telescope.
1946	Rockets first used for scientific observation.
1957	Soviet Union launches the first satellite – Sputnik 1.
1958	U.S.A. launches Explorer 1. The Russians put a dog in orbit.
1961	Yuri Gagarin becomes the first man in space, on Vostok 1.
1962	John Glenn becomes the first American to orbit Earth.
1963	Valentina Tereshkova becomes the first woman in space.
1964	Mariner 4 is the first spacecraft to photograph another planet. It sends 21 pictures of Mars back to Earth.
1965	The Russian cosmonaut Leonov makes the first walk in space on the second of Russia's Vostok missions.
1967	A Russian cosmonaut is killed in Soyuz 1. Three American astronauts are killed in the Apollo 1 launch pad fire. The Russian spacecraft Venera 4 lands on Venus.
1969	The Americans Neil Armstrong and Edwin Aldrin are the first men to land on the Moon.
1970	The Russians obtain data from an instrument package on Venus.
1973	Skylab is launched and visited by three teams of three astronauts. Pioneer 10 takes first close-up photographs of Jupiter.
1974	Mariner 10 photographs Mercury and Venus.
1975	U.S. Apollo and Russian Soyuz manned spacecraft link up in space. Veneras 9 and 10 land on Venus and take photographs.
1976	Viking spacecraft land on Mars but find no sign of life.
1979	Voyagers 1 and 2 fly by Jupiter and its moons.
1980	Voyager 1 takes first close-up photographs of Saturn.
1981	Space shuttle makes first orbital flight.
1982	Space shuttle launches first satellite.
1984	Satellite taken from orbit, repaired and returned to orbit by shuttle astronauts for the first time.
1986	Voyager 2 probe visits Uranus. Shuttle Challenger explodes just after lift-off, killing seven astronauts. Russian Mir space station launched. Halley's comet visited by several spacecraft.
1987	Kvant module added to the Mir space station. Pioneer 10 leaves the Solar System, going beyond Pluto's orbit.
1987-8	Two cosmonauts live in space for just over a year.
1989	Voyager 2 encounters Neptune, at the time the furthest planet from the Sun.
1989-90	Two more modules added to Mir.

IMPROVING AND STORING GAME PIECES

The pieces for each battlegame are designed to be cut out and used as they are. They will last a long time if you strengthen them with thin card as shown in the illustration below.

The best card to use is the sort that postcards are printed on. Glue the pieces onto the card, either separately or in groups, and carefully cut them out with a craft knife or scissors.

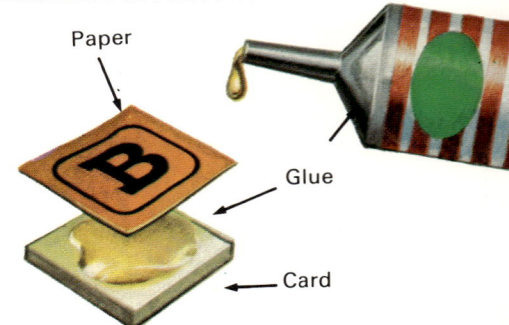

You will need to store the pieces in a safe place, otherwise some will get lost. Use an envelope or a small cardboard box for each game's pieces. Mark the name of the game on the front. Keep all four sets in a drawer or on a shelf.

Making your own pieces

When you are used to playing the games, you may wish to use more exciting and colourful pieces than the paper pieces supplied with this book.

With some practice you can make your own pieces out of card. You can cut them to the shape of the various people and machines in the games. Use your imagination on science-fiction creatures like the Ganoids and the Krul. The illustrations of alien life-forms on pages 24-25 will give you some ideas.

You can also buy miniature figures from model shops to use on the game-boards. You could use models of astronauts for 'Deadly Planet', and space monsters are also available if you look around for them. Small aeroplanes and submarines are useful for 'Invasion Earth!'

One good idea is to turn toothpaste tube tops into spaceships for 'Galactic War'. Start by finding six of these to use as the annihilator ships. You will gradually be able to collect two whole fleets. Spray the ships of the two fleets different colours, and paint portholes on the sides.

PULL-OUT SECTION

The next ten pages include boards and cut-out pieces for four battlegames. To remove them, open the staples in the middle of the book and lift out all these pages. Then close the staples to keep the rest of the book intact.

Cut-out game pieces for **'Space Pirates'** and **'Deadly Planet'** are on the other side of this page.

THE PIECES FOR SPACE PIRATES

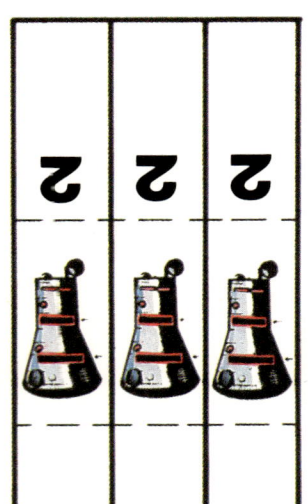

1 = GREATER SPACE ENTERPRISES
2 = MARS AND OUTER PLANETS CONSORTIUM
3 = BOOM-OR-BUST PROSPECTORS
4 = TEXAS-IN-THE-SKY INC.

CUT THESE SLITS. ORE MARKERS CAN BE CARRIED ON THE SPACESHIPS. LIKE THIS

ASSEMBLE THE PIECES LIKE THIS. FIX WITH TAPE

SPACESHIPS OF THE FOUR MINING COMPANIES

ORE MARKERS   M = MAGNESIUM   S = SILICON   T = TITANIUM   Z = ZIRCONIUM

PLANET EARTH

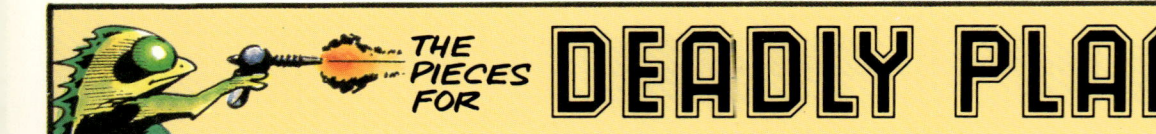

THE PIECES FOR DEADLY PLANET

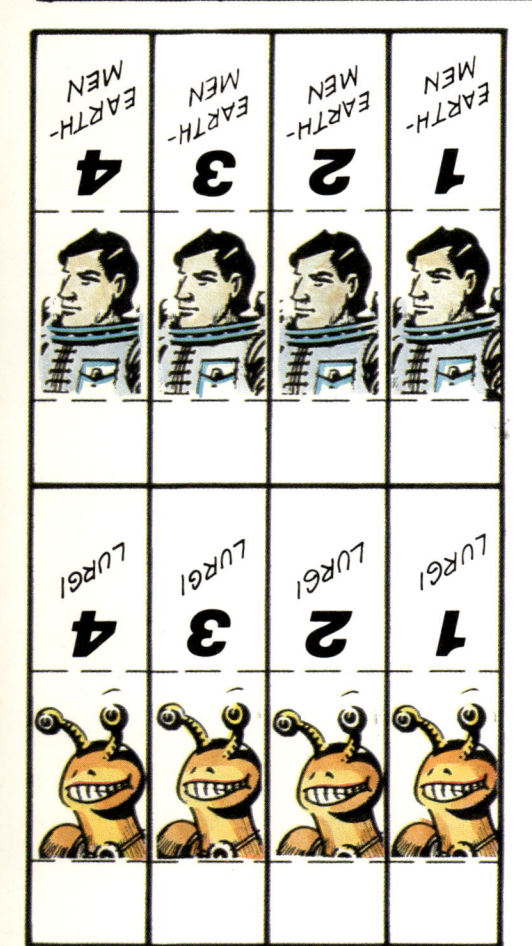

EARTHMEN / LURGI / VEGANS / KALTH-ARIANS

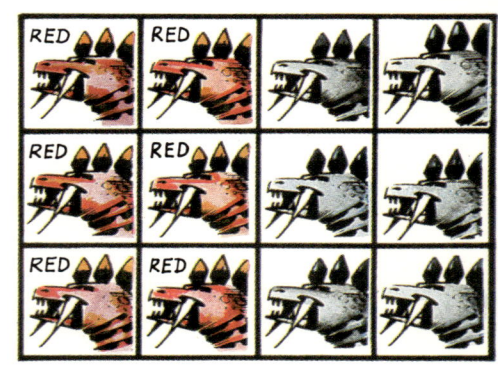

GLAGONS — RED GLAGONS ARE MARKED; OTHERS ARE BLACK GLAGONS

ASTRONAUTS

SENTANT

The board for **'Galactic War'** is on the other side. Remove it with the rest of the pull-out section by opening the staples in the middle of the book. You could use thin card to strengthen this board and make it last longer. Cut some card the same size as the board and then glue it to the plain side. You could also cover it with transparent, sticky-backed plastic.

GALACTIC

KRUL TECHNOLOGY RATING

30 29 28 27 26 25 24 23 22 21 20 19 18 17 16 15 14 13 12 11 10 9 8 7 6 -5 4 3 2 1 0

KRUL HEADQUARTERS PLANET 5

1

1

2

1

1

3

3

4

4

1

1

2

1

KRUL BASE PLANET 5

STELLAR FEDERATION BASE PLANET 5

2

Anti-matter cloud movement reminder

6 1 2
5 4 3

The board for **'Deadly Planet'** is on the other side. Remove it with the rest of the pull-out section by opening the staples in the middle of the book. You could use thin card to strengthen this board and make it last longer. Cut some card the same size as the board and then glue it to the plain side. You could also cover it with transparent, sticky-backed plastic.

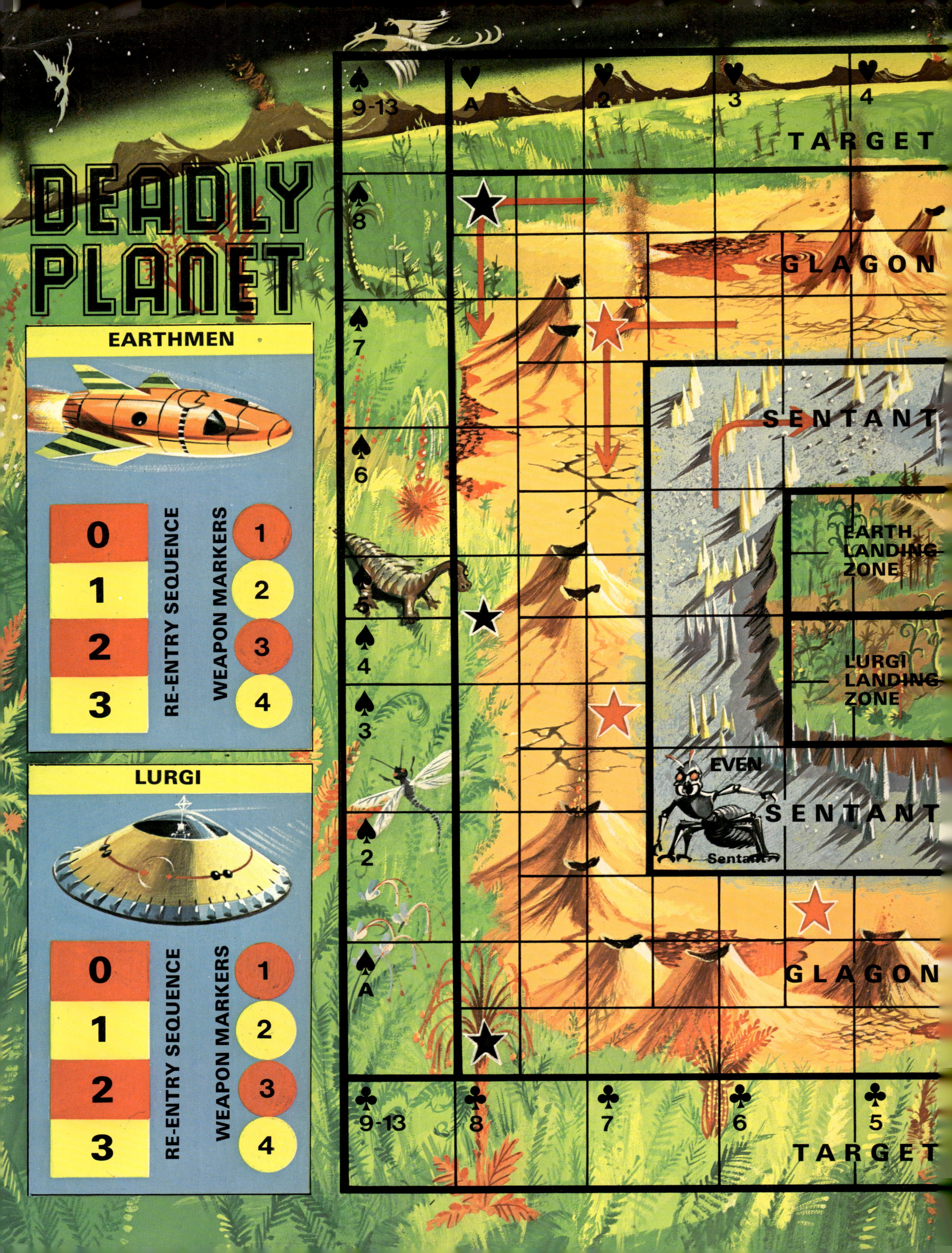

DEADLY PLANET

EARTHMEN

RE-ENTRY SEQUENCE	WEAPON MARKERS
0	1
1	2
2	3
3	4

LURGI

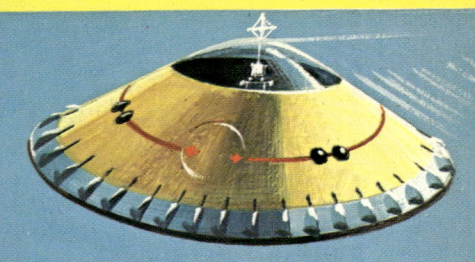

RE-ENTRY SEQUENCE	WEAPON MARKERS
0	1
1	2
2	3
3	4

♠ 9-13 | ♥ A | ♥ 2 | ♥ 3 | ♥ 4
♠ 8
♠ 7
♠ 6
♠ 5
♠ 4
♠ 3
♠ 2
♠ A
♣ 9-13 | ♣ 8 | ♣ 7 | ♣ 6 | ♣ 5

TARGET
GLAGON
SENTANT
EARTH LANDING ZONE
LURGI LANDING ZONE
EVEN SENTANT
GLAGON
TARGET

The board for **'Space Pirates'** is on the other side. Remove it with the rest of the pull-out section by opening the staples in the middle of the book. You could use thin card to strengthen this board and make it last longer. Cut some card the same size as the board and then glue it to the plain side. You could also cover it with transparent, sticky-backed plastic.

SPACE

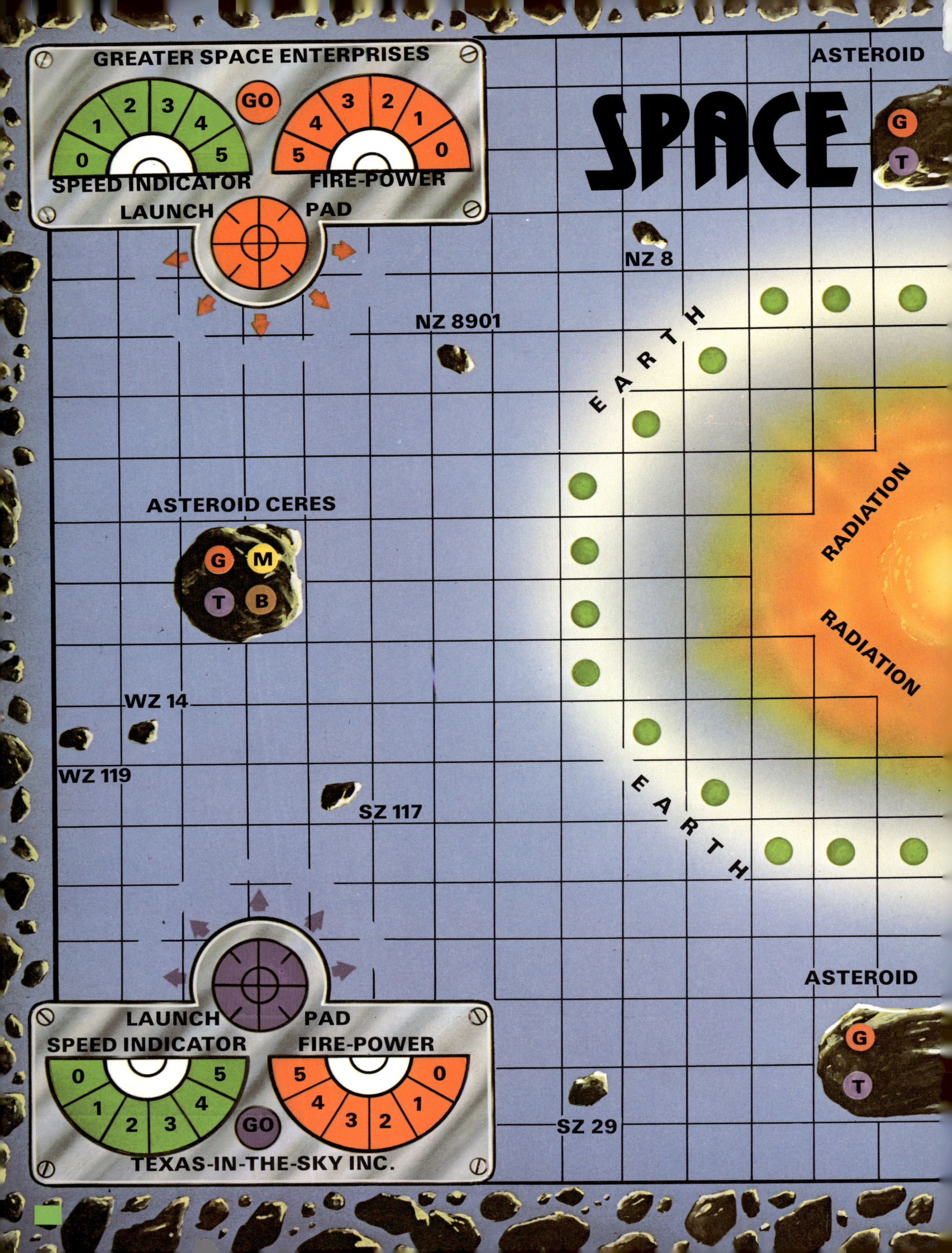

GREATER SPACE ENTERPRISES

SPEED INDICATOR: 0 1 2 3 4 5 — GO
FIRE-POWER: 5 4 3 2 1 0

LAUNCH PAD

ASTEROID — G T

NZ 8

NZ 8901

EARTH

RADIATION

RADIATION

ASTEROID CERES — G M T B

WZ 14

WZ 119

SZ 117

EARTH

SZ 29

ASTEROID — G T

LAUNCH PAD
SPEED INDICATOR: 0 1 2 3 4 5
FIRE-POWER: 5 4 3 2 1 0 — GO

TEXAS-IN-THE-SKY INC.

The board for **'Invasion Earth!'** is on the other side. Remove it with the rest of the pull-out section by opening the staples in the middle of the book. You could use thin card to strengthen this board and make it last longer. Cut some card the same size as the board and then glue it to the plain side. You could also cover it with transparent, sticky-backed plastic.

TRACK OF ORBITING

1 2 3 4 5 6 7 8

U.S.S.R.

VLADIVOSTOK BASE

HAWAIIAN ISLANDS

HAWAII BASE

GILBERT ISLANDS

NEW GUINEA

SAMOA

NEW HEBRIDES

AUSTRALIA

SYDNEY BASE

NEW ZEALAND

INVASION EARTH!

MISSILE SATELLITES

9 10 11 12 13 14 15 16

CANADA

SAN DIEGO BASE

UNITED STATES OF AMERICA

TUAMOTU ARCHIPELAGO

GALAPAGOS ISLANDS

SOUTH AMERICA

EASTER ISLAND

PIRATES

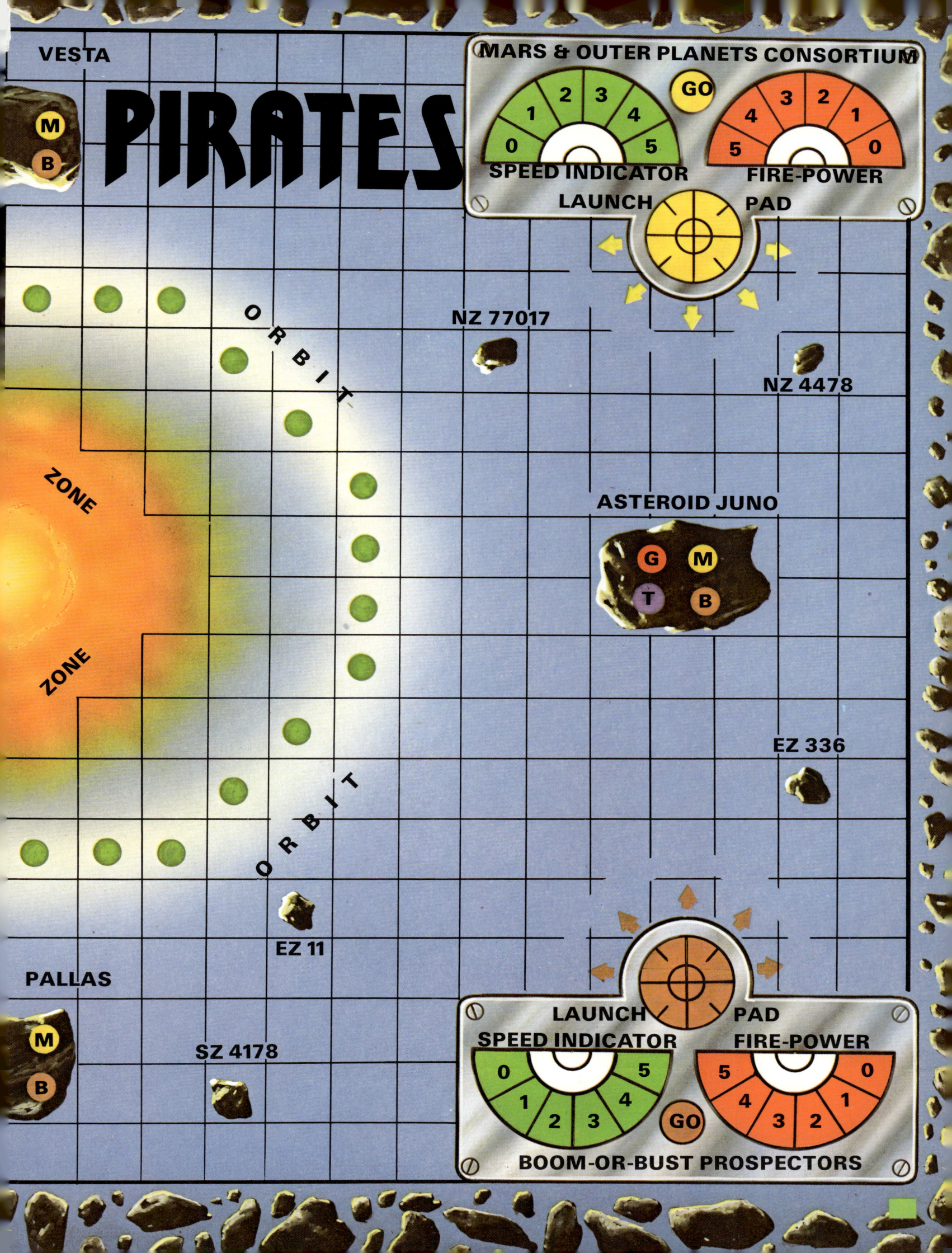

VESTA

MARS & OUTER PLANETS CONSORTIUM

SPEED INDICATOR: 0 1 2 3 4 5 GO
FIRE-POWER: 5 4 3 2 1 0
LAUNCH PAD

ORBIT

NZ 77017

NZ 4478

ZONE

ASTEROID JUNO

ZONE

EZ 336

ORBIT

EZ 11

PALLAS

SZ 4178

LAUNCH PAD
SPEED INDICATOR: 0 1 2 3 4 5
FIRE-POWER: 5 4 3 2 1 0
GO

BOOM-OR-BUST PROSPECTORS

ZONE
♥ 5 | ♥ 6 | ♥ 7 | ♥ 8 | ♥ 9-13

ZONE
♦ A

ZONE
♦ 2

ZONE
ODD Sentant
♦ 3

VEGAN LANDING ZONE
♦ 4

KALTHARIAN LANDING ZONE
♦ 5

♦ 6

♦ 7

ZONE
♦ 8

♦ 9-13

ZONE
♣ 4 | ♣ 3 | ♣ 2 | ♣ A

VEGANS

RE-ENTRY SEQUENCE	WEAPON MARKERS
0	1
1	2
2	3
3	4

KALTHARIANS

RE-ENTRY SEQUENCE	WEAPON MARKERS
0	1
1	2
2	3
3	4

WAR
A GAME FOR TWO PLAYERS

STELLAR FEDERATION TECHNOLOGY RATING

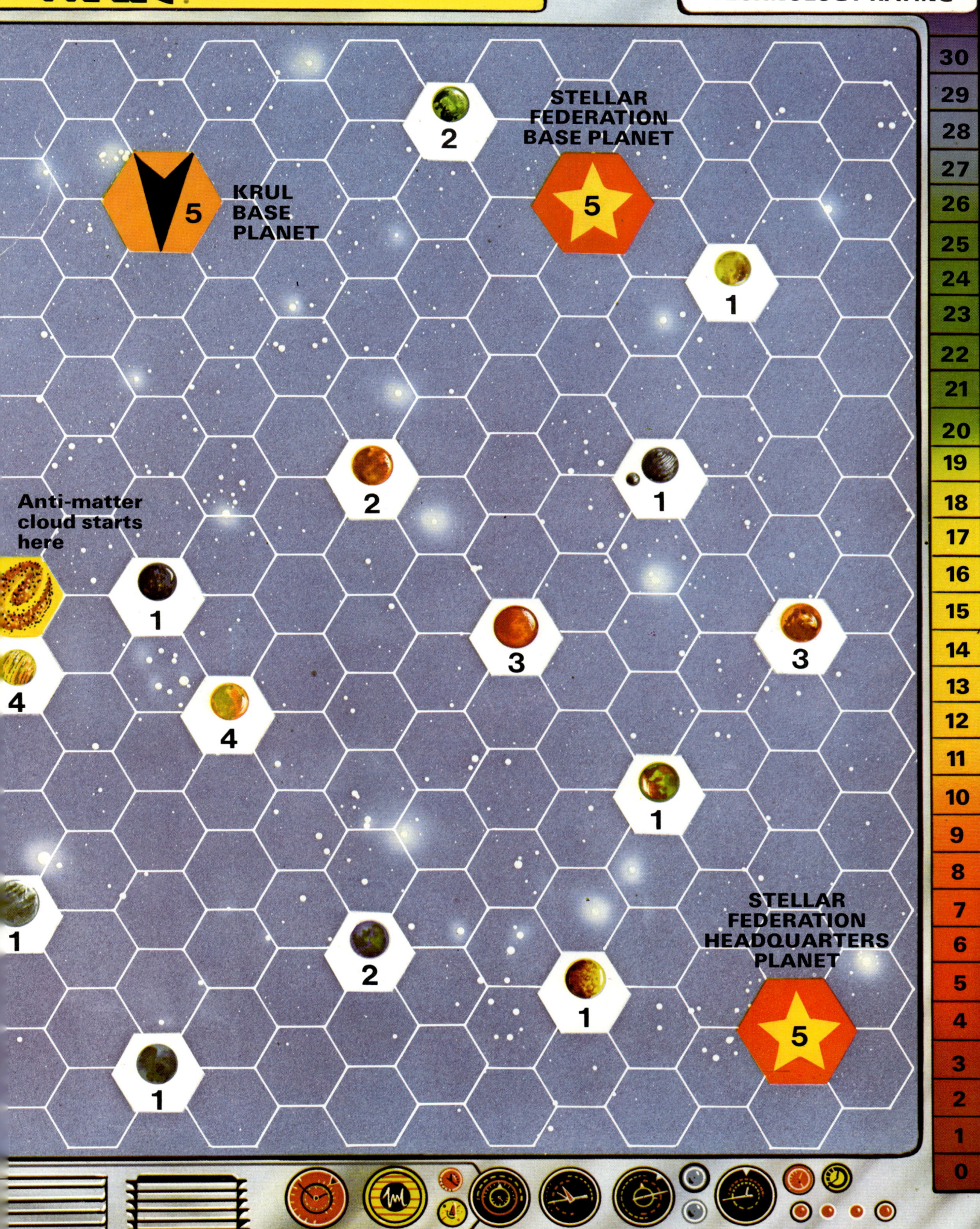

KRUL BASE PLANET

STELLAR FEDERATION BASE PLANET

Anti-matter cloud starts here

STELLAR FEDERATION HEADQUARTERS PLANET

THE PIECES FOR INVASION EARTH!

AIR FLEET — 4
HYDROFOIL — 4
SUBMARINE — 2
SUBMARINE — 2
SPARE

ORBITING MISSILE SATELLITES — EARTH FORCES

BEACON SPACESHIPS (SHOWING THE GANOID PILOT) — all value 2

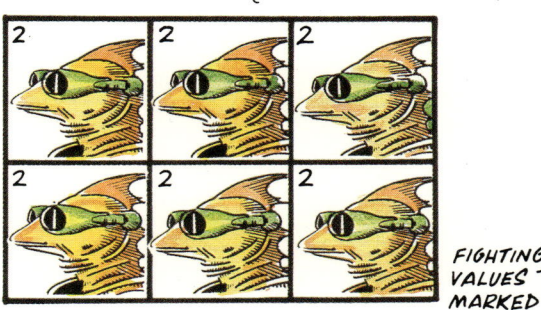

SPAWNING CRAFT — fighting values marked on the corners (all value 1), plus SPARE

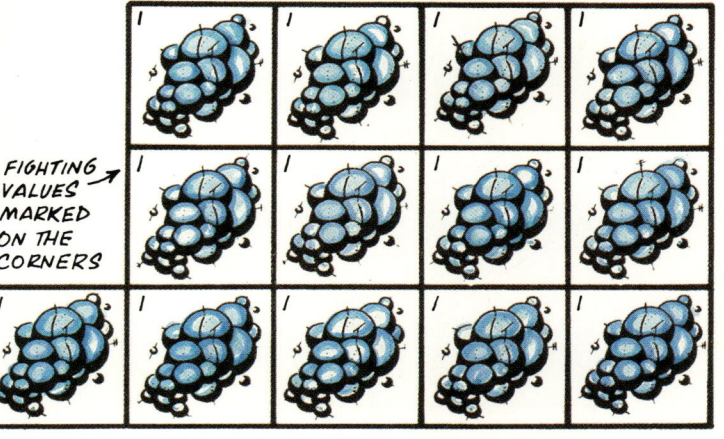

USE THIS SPINNER IF YOU DO NOT HAVE A DICE

SHARPENED MATCHSTICK

THE PIECES FOR GALACTIC WAR

KRUL STARSHIPS

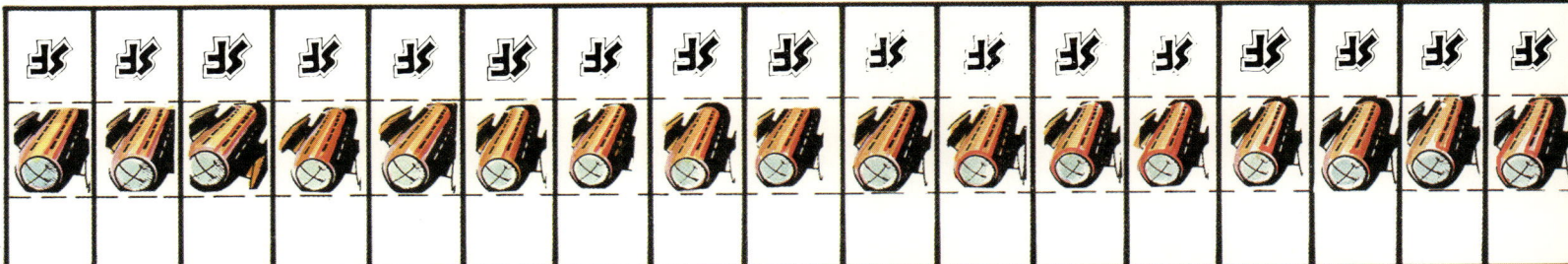

STELLAR FEDERATION STARSHIPS — 5F

KRUL ANNIHILATORS

STELLAR FEDERATION ANNIHILATORS

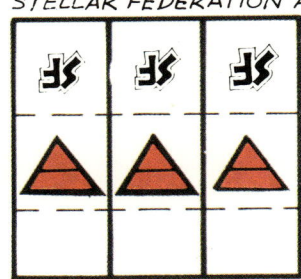

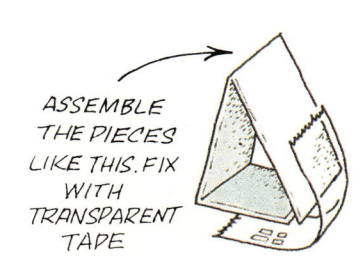

ANTI-MATTER CLOUD — ASSEMBLE THE PIECES LIKE THIS. FIX WITH TRANSPARENT TAPE

Cut-out game pieces for **'Invasion Earth!'** and **'Galactic War'** are on the other side of this page. Remove them with the rest of the pull-out section by opening the staples in the middle of the book.

THE RULES FOR SPACE PIRATES

A game for two, three or four players.

A.D. 2076. Rival companies are competing to exploit the mineral wealth of the Asteroid Belt between Mars and Jupiter. They will stop at nothing to get the precious ores to Earth first.

1 The pieces

4 ZIRCONIUM ORE MARKERS, PLACED ON	JUNO	EACH COMPANY HAS ONE OF EACH MARKER TYPE TO BE COLLECTED FROM EACH ASTEROID.
4 TITANIUM " "	PALLAS	
4 SILICON " "	CERES	
4 MAGNESIUM " "	VESTA	

12 SPACESHIPS — 3 FOR EACH COMPANY

1 PLANET EARTH — MOVES 1 SPACE AROUND ITS ORBIT PATH AFTER EACH PLAYERS TURN.

2 Extras
A dice
2 used matchsticks for each player

3 Object of the game
Each player controls one company.
Companies send spacecraft from their bases to collect mineral loads from asteroids Juno, Ceres, Vesta and Pallas. They then have to land the minerals safely on Earth.
The first player to land his company's four mineral loads on Earth wins the game.

4 Setting up the pieces
Each player takes three spaceships and four ore markers. He places one spaceship on his company's launch pad, and keeps the others in reserve on the side of the board. He puts each ore marker on the asteroid rich in its mineral, e.g. the zirconium card on asteroid Juno.
Place the Earth on the black-framed square in its orbit path.
Players use matchsticks as pointers, to mark their speed and fire-power on the indicators provided. Each player starts with the speed marker set at **0** and the fire-power marker at **5**.

5 Playing the game
Players take turns to move. Throw the dice to decide who goes first. The player who throws the highest number starts, and play then passes clockwise round the board.
Each player can have only one spaceship on the board at a time. The order of play in each player's turn is:
1 Move the spaceship (see **6**)
2 Attack another spaceship, if required (see **8**)
3 Move the Earth one square clockwise around its orbit (see **9**).

6 Moving
Spaceships can move in any direction. Their speed is shown on the speed indicator.
Spaceships **must** either speed up or slow down each turn, increasing or decreasing their speed level by 1. Choose which you prefer to do, move the indicator up or down one number, and then move the spaceship the number of squares shown.

Spaceships cannot move into the deadly radiation zone around the Sun, or through squares occupied by small asteroids (EZ 336, NZ 8901 etc.) or other spacecraft.

7 Take-off and landing
To take off
1 At rest on its launch pad or on a planet or asteroid, the spaceship's speed indicator is at 0.
2 Increase speed indicator to 1, move spaceship one square into space.
3 Speed up to 2 in the following turn, and proceed normally.

To land
1 Slow down speed to 1. At this point you must be one square away from your landing square so you can move straight onto the asteroid or planet.
2 In the next turn move onto the landing square and slow down the speed to 0. You have landed.

Spaceships can carry one or two mineral loads, but no more.
Once mineral loads have been landed on Earth they are removed from the board. The spaceship can then go to get the others.

8 Attacking
Spaceships can attack enemy spacecraft within a range of two squares. No spaceship can make an attack while it is on Earth. Only one attack is allowed each turn.
The attacking player throws the dice. The results of the attack are decided as follows:

ATTACKER ADDS UP: DICE THROW & FIRE-POWER RATING

DEFENDER ADDS UP: SPEED-LEVEL & FIRE-POWER RATING

If the attacker has the higher total, he scores a hit. If his total is the same or less than the defender's, he has missed and play continues. Whether he hits or misses, the attacker reduces his fire-power rating by 1 every time he fires a shot.

When a spaceship has been hit, it goes out of control for **2 turns**. It continues to move in the direction of its last move at the speed shown on its indicator when it was hit. Any ship that crashes into an asteroid, the Sun's radiation zone, or the debris around the edge of the board, is destroyed and removed from the board. A substitute spaceship can then be brought into play from the player's launch pad. Any player who loses all three of his spaceships drops out of the game.

If the wrecked spaceship is carrying an ore marker, the marker is placed back on its asteroid. It has to be collected again.

When a spaceship's fire-power rating drops to 0, it can return to its launch pad for new weapons. Its rating then moves up to 5 again.

9 The Earth
The Earth moves 1 square clockwise round its orbit at the end of **each** player's turn.
The Earth is surrounded by a police patrol zone which operates within a range of 2 squares from Earth in all directions (see diagram).

Spaceships carrying out attacks within the police patrol zone are arrested and held on Earth for two moves. Their weapons are confiscated, and their fire-power rating falls to 0. To re-arm, they must fly back to their bases for fresh weapons.
Any ship that comes within the Earth police patrol zone while out of control is rescued and lands on Earth.
Spaceships landed on Earth move round its orbit with it.

10 Tips on tactics
● Slow your spaceship down and steer it away from danger zones if you expect it to be attacked, to reduce the danger of it being destroyed.
● Once you have got the hang of the game, try playing it using two, or all three, of your spaceships at the same time.
● Earth is difficult to land on because (as in real life) it is moving all the time. The best way to land is to end your move at a speed of 1, 4 squares in front of the Earth in its orbit path. The three other players' turns will move it towards your spaceship.

17

THE RULES FOR DEADLY PLANET

A game for two, three or four players.

Four races are competing for control of a wild planet. Several kinds of animals already live on it – like the ferocious Sentant and the tamer but still dangerous Glagons.

To prevent the four races from going to war with each other, the Stellar Federation decides to grant the planet to the race whose astronauts manage to beat the problems of living on it and reach selected points in a Target Zone on the planet's surface first.

1 The Pieces

PIECE	MOVES
4 EARTHMEN	1 SPACE PER TURN
4 VEGANS	
4 KALTHARIANS	
4 LURGI	
1 SENTANT	AROUND THE SENTANT ZONE
6 RED GLAGONS	AROUND THE GLAGON ZONE
6 BLACK GLAGONS	

2 Extras
A pack of cards
A dice
4 counters for each player

3 Object of the game
Before the game starts, four cards are dealt to each player. The cards show the spaces in the Target Zone that each player's astronauts must head for.

The first player to get his four astronauts to the squares shown on his cards wins the game. Jacks, Queens and Kings count as 11, 12 and 13 respectively.

Once an astronaut has reached a target square, he is safe, and can be taken off the board.

4 Setting up the board
One player deals the target cards. Each player keeps his cards face up on the table.

Each player places his four astronauts on the four squares of his landing zone, and puts 1 counter on each of the four weapon spaces marked next to his spaceship.

Put the six Red Glagons on the six squares in the Glagon Zone marked with red stars, and the six Black Glagons on the squares marked with black stars.

Throw the dice to decide which square the Sentant is to start from. If it shows an odd number, it starts from the Sentant starting-square marked 'odd'; if even, from the starting-square marked 'even'.

ORDER OF PLAY
- EARTHMEN
- VEGANS
- SENTANT (DICE THROW)
- KALTHARIANS
- LURGI
- GLAGONS (DICE THROW)

5 Playing the game
Players take turns to move. The Earthmen go first, followed by the Vegans, the Kaltharians and the Lurgi in that order.

Each player can move all, some or none of his pieces each turn.

All astronauts move 1 square in any direction, except when riding Glagons (see 7).

Two astronauts cannot occupy the same square.
Diagonal moves are not allowed.

The large squares in the Sentant Zone and on the outer edge of the Glagon Zone count as 1 square, just the same as the smaller squares elsewhere on the board.

6 The Sentant Zone
The Sentant moves **clockwise** around the Sentant Zone. The number of squares it moves is decided by throwing the dice at the end of the **Vegan** player's turn.

Any astronaut on a square on which the Sentant lands is attacked by it, and must retreat immediately to his spaceship to recover.

Place the wounded astronaut on square 0 of the Re-entry Sequence, marked on the board next to his spaceship. For the next three turns, the astronaut moves 1 square each turn along the Sequence, re-entering his player's landing zone after leaving square 3 of the Sequence.

7 The Glagon Zone
The Glagons move **anti-clockwise** around the Glagon Zone. They move after the **Lurgi** player's move. He throws the dice to find out how many squares to move them.

Astronauts can only cross the Glagon Zone by 'riding' Glagons.

They must wait in the Sentant Zone to catch a Glagon. An astronaut can 'mount' a Glagon by moving on top of it when it stops in an adjoining square.

The astronaut then remains on the Glagon until after the Glagons' move. The Glagon he is 'riding' moves the same number of squares as the other Glagons, but in a direction chosen by its 'rider'. If the dice shows, say, a 5, he can move his Glagon 5 squares in the direction he wants to go, **finishing on a target zone square.**

If the Glagon does not move enough squares for the astronaut to reach the Target Zone, the astronaut is 'thrown' by it. He must immediately return to his spaceship to recover. For recovery rules, see **6**.

Astronauts can only spend 1 turn on a Glagon.

An astronaut can, however, use his move to return to an empty square in the Sentant Zone.

Red Glagons return to the nearest unoccupied square on the inner border of their zone as soon as their rider leaves them.

Black Glagons stay on the outer border of their zone.

RED GLAGONS MOVE BACK TO THEIR INNER ZONE

8 Weapons
Each astronaut has a gamma gun. This is represented on the board by his weapon counter. Gamma guns can be fired **once only.** Once an astronaut has fired his gun, remove the counter from the board (e.g. Lurgi Weapon Marker 1 when Lurgi 1 has fired) to show that that astronaut cannot fire again.

Gamma guns have a range of **1** square (diagonal shots are not allowed). They disable the astronaut they are aimed at, and he must return immediately to his spaceship to recover (see **6**).

If an astronaut has reached his target square without using his gun, it can be transferred to any of his team-mates that do not have a weapon.

9 Tips on tactics
● Use Black Glagons whenever possible to move quickly round the Target Zone.
● Save your gamma guns to knock out rivals who are getting near to their targets.

THE RULES FOR INVASION EARTH!

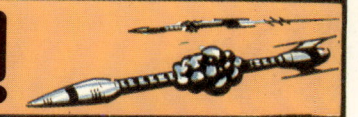

Invasion Earth is a short game for two players that takes about half an hour to play.

The Ganoids, a race of sea creatures whose planet is slowly drying up, are seeking new worlds to breed on. Earth Command learns from monitor satellites that they have despatched a force to establish trial spawning-grounds in the Pacific Ocean. Faced by this threat to the Earth ecosystem, Command leaders send a search-and-destroy task-force to the trouble area. Can their fleets hunt down the invaders before they multiply beyond control?

1 The pieces

PIECES	MOVES (PER TURN)	FIGHTING VALUE (F.V.)
EARTH COMMAND		
1 AIR FLEET	UP TO 3 SQUARES	4
1 HYDROFOIL FLEET	UP TO 2 SQUARES	4
2 SUBMARINE FLEETS	UP TO 1 SQUARE	2
3 ORBITING MISSILE SATELLITES (OMS)	1 SPACE ALONG THE ORBITAL TRACK	
GANOIDS		
6 BEACON SPACESHIPS	ANYWHERE ON THE BOARD EXCEPT EARTH BASES	2
16 SPAWNING CRAFT	CANNOT MOVE ONCE PLACED ON BOARD	1

ORBITING MISSILE SATELLITES

OMS'S THREATEN ONLY THE COLUMN THEY ARE OVER AT THE BEGINNING OF EACH TURN

2 Object of the game
The Ganoids plan to breed in the depths of the Pacific Ocean by releasing spawn from submerged spacecraft. To win the game, the Ganoids have to submerge either **10** separate spawning craft, or **8** spawning craft in a group. Like this:

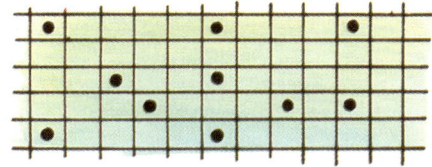

10 separate craft

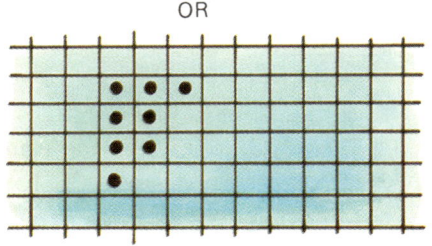

OR

8 grouped craft (but not necessarily in this pattern)

The Earth Command player wins by hunting down and destroying the Ganoid craft before they can do this.

3 Setting up the pieces
The Earth Command player places his fleets in the four Earth Command bases, one fleet in each base. The three orbiting missile satellites (OMS) are placed on positions 1, 6 and 11 of their track.

The Ganoid player starts the game with all his pieces on the side of the board. He takes the first turn.

4 Playing the game
The Ganoid player starts by placing one beacon spaceship on the board on any square except Earth Command bases.

The Earth Command player then takes his turn. He can move all, some or none of his fleets each turn. Moves are listed in **1**.

Earth Command pieces do **not** move diagonally.

In following turns the Ganoid player can do these things:
1 Place one new beacon ship on the board.
2 Move beacon ships already on the board.
3 Place one or two spawning craft on beacon ships already in place (see **5**).
4 Submerge spawning craft that can do so (see **5**).

5 Landing and submerging
It takes three turns for the Ganoid player to submerge a craft:
Turn 1
Place a beacon spaceship on an unoccupied square.
Turn 2
Land a spawning craft on top of the beacon ship.
Turn 3
Submerge the spawning craft. Do this by turning it upside down.
The beacon ship can now leave the square in the same turn.

Submerged spawning craft can **only** be attacked by submarine fleets and OMSs.

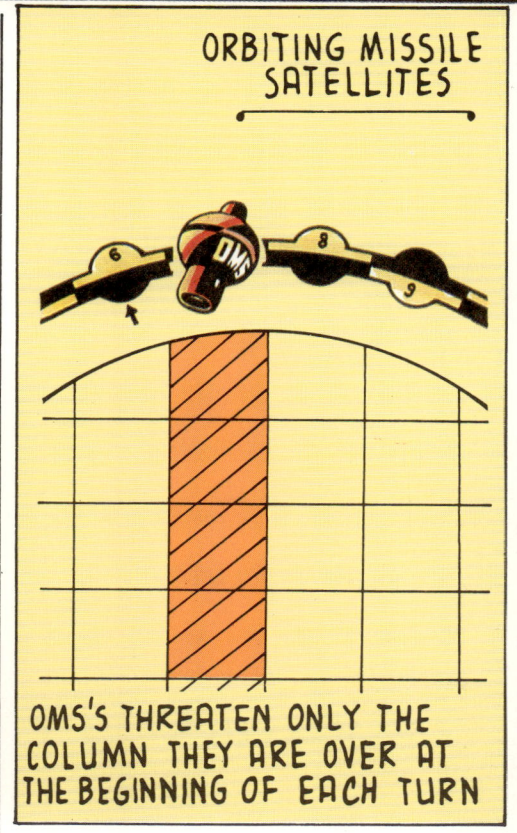

6 Earth command attacks
Only Earth Command pieces can make attacks; the Ganoids can defend themselves, but are not equipped to attack.

To make an attack, the Earth Command player has to move a piece (or pieces) onto a Ganoid-occupied square.

He can only do this if the Ganoids have a **lower** total fighting value than his own forces.

The Ganoid pieces on the square are destroyed and removed from the board.

7 The orbiting missile satellites (OMS)
The OMS all move one position along their track each turn, starting again from 1 when they leave position 16. They move after the Earth Command player has finished his turn. They cannot be used for attacks until the following turn.

Each OMS has a single homing missile that can be used by the Earth Command player to destroy **all** pieces in one square in the row of squares directly beneath it. Once its missile has been used, the OMS is removed from the board.

OMSs can be used to destroy submerged craft as well as those on the surface.

8 Tips on tactics
● The Earth Command player must try to keep at least one fleet within easy reach of every part of the board.
● The Ganoids should try to submerge spawning craft at the edges of the board, as far as possible from Earth Command forces.
● After you have played the game a few times, try making it harder for the Ganoid player by giving Earth Command more OMSs.

THE RULES FOR GALACTIC WAR

A game for two players

A.D. 3000. Krul invaders from the Andromeda Galaxy have established a foothold in a little-known sector of our own Milky Way Galaxy, and are preparing for total war. The Stellar Federation has gathered all available forces on base planets in the sector to meet the threat. The future of the Milky Way depends on the outcome of their struggle.

ANTI-MATTER CLOUD

THIS MOVES 2 SPACES IN THE DIRECTIONS SHOWN WHEN THE DICE IS THROWN

1 The pieces

PIECE		MOVES
STELLAR FEDERATION	17 STARSHIPS	1 SPACE PER TURN
	3 ANNIHILATOR SHIPS	1 SPACE " "
THE KRUL INVADERS	17 STARSHIPS	" "
	3 ANNIHILATOR SHIPS	" "
1 ANTI-MATTER CLOUD		2 SPACES IN THE DIRECTION SHOWN BY DICE THROW

2 Extras
A dice (or use the spinner provided)
2 counters (to mark technological levels)

3 Object of the game
The Krul and Stellar Federation both aim to send a fleet to capture the enemy's headquarters planet.
The first player to capture the planet wins the game. A fleet of at least 5 ships is needed to do this.

4 Starting the game
Each player starts the game with his starship pieces at the side of the board. Place the anti-matter cloud on the space marked near the centre of the board.
Put technology rating markers on '0'.
The Krul player starts.

5 Moving
Starships enter the board through H.Q. and base planets. In the first turn, each player can move one ship into each of his three H.Q. and base planets.
In following turns, players can:
1 Bring fresh starships onto the board on base or H.Q. planets. If the base is already occupied, the starship on it and all others linked to it move out 1 space to make room for the newcomer; **and**
2 Move each ship or fleet of ships 1 space in any direction
Only one starship can occupy a space at a time.

6 Technology levels
Each side has a technology rating, measured on the scales provided at the edges of the board.
The planets scattered around the board have different technology levels, shown by the number on their space. Players' ratings rise or fall as they capture or lose planets.
H.Q. and base planets have a technology level of 5, so as soon as a player has occupied all three of them he can set his technology level at 15.

7 Capturing planets
To capture a planet, a player must send a fleet of starships to it. To capture a planet with a technology level of 4, a fleet of at least 4 ships must be sent; for a technology level of 3, 3 ships, etc.
A player who captures a planet adds its technology level to his own. He moves the marker up his technology scale by a corresponding number of points – for instance, 3 for a planet with a level of 3.
To keep control of a captured planet, a player must leave a starship on it. If the starship abandons the planet, its technology level is deducted from the player's rating on the technology scale.
Base and H.Q. planets are held and captured in the same way as other planets.

8 Attacking
At the end of his move, a player can attack enemy ships on spaces next to one of his own starships.
Both players throw the dice. Then they each add up:

DICE THROW
+
NUMBER OF SHIPS IN THE FLEET
+
TECHNOLOGY RATING

The player with the higher total wins. The losing craft is destroyed, and the piece is removed from the board. The winning starship remains in place.
In case of a tie, both ships retreat one space.
If a whole fleet moves into an attack position, only one of the ships in it can actually attack. One attack is allowed for each fleet each turn (e.g. a player with four fleets could make a maximum of four attacks).

9 The anti-matter cloud
The anti-matter cloud moves at random through space, obliterating starships in its path. Planets have anti-matter neutralizers, so they are unaffected.
To determine the cloud's move, the dice is thrown at the end of the Stellar Federation player's turn. The cloud then moves **2** spaces in the direction shown.

10 Annihilators
Each player has three annihilator ships. These are starships with built-in nuclear bombs that can be triggered to explode by the player the ship belongs to at any time in the game. The annihilator destroys all pieces, friendly and hostile (including itself), within a range of **1** space (see diagram).

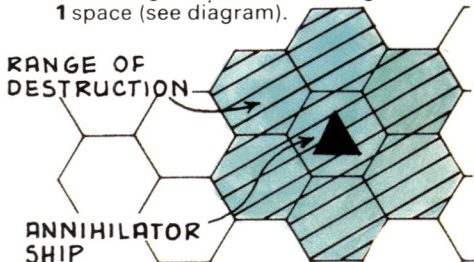

RANGE OF DESTRUCTION

ANNIHILATOR SHIP

The annihilators otherwise move and act like other spacecraft. They explode if attacked **and defeated** by an enemy starship.

11 Tips on tactics
● Build up a high technology level by setting out to capture the most highly rated planets, and by trying to capture enemy base planets.
● Build a strong fleet as quickly as you can to launch a direct attack on the enemy H.Q. planet.

12 A simpler game
For a simpler game, launch starships onto the board only through the H.Q. planets. Use base planets simply as ordinary planets, each with a rating of 5.

THE WEALTH ABOVE OUR HEADS

At present we manufacture goods from minerals and other materials found on our own planet. But we are now beginning to run short of some of these. Many of the same materials are found on the Moon. In the future man may mine them and make goods from them on the Moon itself.

Moon-mining

There are advantages in making things on the Moon. The gravity there is only one-sixth what it is on Earth. Mining and building on the Moon will be easier.

Although there is no atmosphere on the Moon there is a lot of oxygen. It is found in the rocks, mixed with the minerals. It will be possible to extract the oxygen.

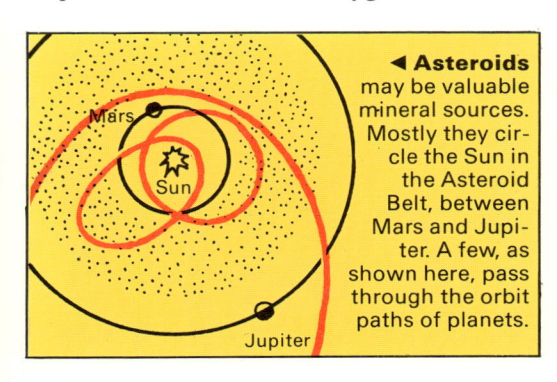

◄ **Asteroids** may be valuable mineral sources. Mostly they circle the Sun in the Asteroid Belt, between Mars and Jupiter. A few, as shown here, pass through the orbit paths of planets.

There is no water on the Moon but water can be made from the gases oxygen and hydrogen. There is no hydrogen on the Moon so it would have to be taken there. This would be difficult at first because it would have to be taken by spacecraft from Earth. But anything taken to the Moon would be used again and again.

It will be easy to use energy from the Sun to provide heat, light and power for living and working on the Moon. Solar cells would be much larger versions of the ones used to power instruments in spacecraft.

Mining the mineral wealth of the Moon will only be a first step. The low gravity may make the Moon the ideal place for making spaceships and space stations. And by the time we are able to do that easily it may be possible to use the asteroids for our needs as well.

Riches of the asteroids

Asteroids are the small rocky bodies orbiting the Sun between Mars and Jupiter. There are thousands of them. They will provide a rich source of raw material. It may be possible to move some of the small ones into the orbit of the Moon or Earth. This might be done by attaching

▲ **You are the pilot** as this 21st-century moonliner comes down at Gagaringrad in the Sea of Rains. This international magnesium-mining base is staffed by Americans and Russians who work underground and in domed refineries.

A 'farm' of solar cells (left centre) stores up enough energy to keep the plant functioning during the Moon's two-week-long night. Supply craft for space cities take off from the track of an electro-magnetic launcher.

rocket motors to them to ease them out of their orbits.

Minerals mined on the Moon and from the asteroids will be used to make light-weight metal plates and girders. These will be the basic units for the spaceships and space stations.

A robot work-force

A lot of the tasks that would be difficult for men to do could be done by robots and other machines. Instead of taking samples of soil from the planets and taking pictures, as robot explorers do now, these machines would be built to dig for minerals. Eventually the machines themselves could build the spaceships and space stations people will need to live in.

Many of the ideas that scientists have now may seem incredible. But they will be quite possible for our descendants.

21

VOYAGE TO THE STARS

It seems likely now that men will one day try to travel to the stars. They will go in search of new planets to live on, away from the overcrowded Earth. They will go in search of knowledge and adventure.

From what we know, a journey to a planet outside our Solar System will take a very long time. To find a suitable planet to land on we may have to travel far beyond the nearest stars. The Apollo spacecraft reached a speed of 40,250kph (25,000mph) on the journey to the Moon. At this speed it would take about 100,000 years to reach Proxima Centauri, the nearest star.

Building starships

The first starships to be built would be much faster than the Apollo craft. But they are not likely to go at anything like the speed of light. So they will take hundreds of years to reach stars with planets on which people can settle.

This does not matter if the spaceships are built to last long enough, and if the people on board are prepared to live, have children and die on the spaceship.

Colonies on the stars

A 'multi-generation' expedition like this, planning to start a colony at the end of its long journey, would have to be very large – at least 2,000 people. If there were fewer the colony would not be able to produce enough strong children. Several starships could travel in a fleet to make up the numbers.

Refuelling in space

Starships will have to be very big to hold from 200 to 2000 people each. One possible model would be powered by nuclear engines using a hydrogen fuel. Hydrogen is the most common element in the Universe. The star travellers would be able to refuel from hydrogen-rich planets like our Jupiter on their journey.

The star travellers might sleep during the long journey, rather as an animal hibernates in the winter. An autopilot would control the spaceship and wake up the passengers when a likely planet had been reached. Or there could be some passengers asleep and some awake.

The spaceships of the future would be assembled in space. They would be made of materials invented for use in space. They will use engines that work best in space. These would not have to be as massive as those needed to lift the Apollo spacecraft off the Earth.

One engine that has been projected would use nuclear fission to create great heat. Hydrogen heated in this way would provide enormous thrust.

Another sort of engine using nuclear power might explode tiny hydrogen bombs behind the spaceship, creating the thrust directly. There would be a rapid chain of small explosions and each one would push the spaceship forward.

Photon sails

Scientists have thought of other ways of powering starships, using the knowledge they have at the moment. Some think that thrust could be obtained by using photons – particles of light – in huge 'photon-sail' spaceships. An ion-powered rocket might also be used. Electrically charged atoms would provide the thrust as they were electrostatically repulsed from the engine.

The asteroids in the Asteroid Belt might be used as spaceships. The asteroids could be hollowed out and fitted with motors and life support systems for hundreds of people to live in.

The longest journey

Space travel to the stars is probably a long way off. There are no pressures on man at the moment so great that he has to leave the planet. But at some time in the future he may want or need to go somewhere else. Then the first starships will be built – to make the most adventurous journey of all.

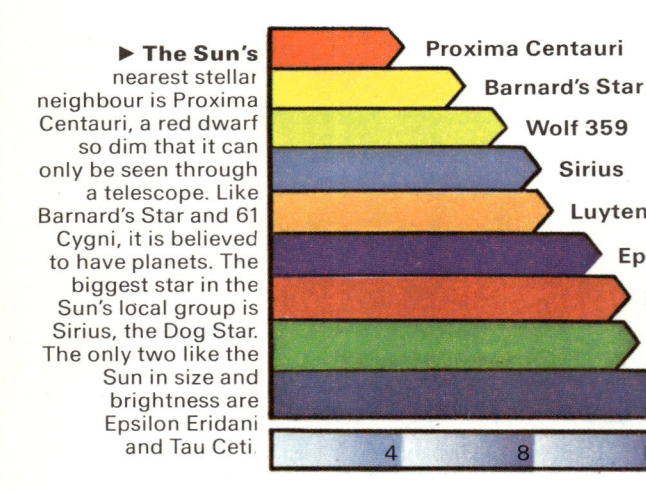

▶ The Sun's nearest stellar neighbour is Proxima Centauri, a red dwarf so dim that it can only be seen through a telescope. Like Barnard's Star and 61 Cygni, it is believed to have planets. The biggest star in the Sun's local group is Sirius, the Dog Star. The only two like the Sun in size and brightness are Epsilon Eridani and Tau Ceti.

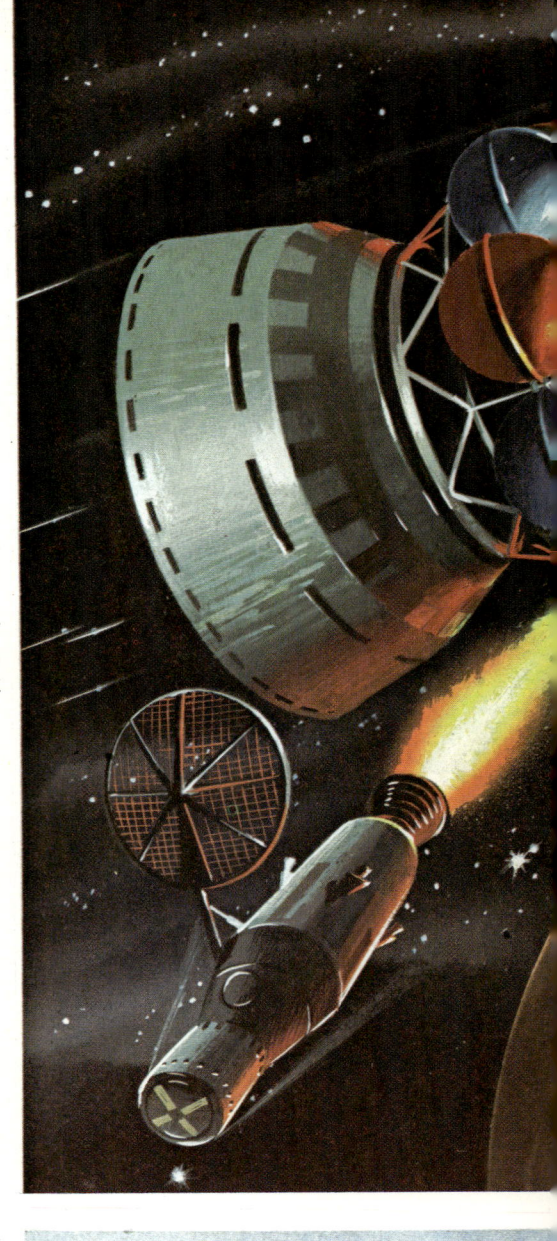

- Proxima Centauri
- Barnard's Star
- Wolf 359
- Sirius
- Luytens 726-8
- Epsilon Eridani
- Epsilon Indi
- 61 Cygni
- Tau Ceti

4   8   12   Light years from the Sun

Interstellar Ramjet

A ramjet speeds through space. The vessel carries 500 colonists, who are kept in hibernation chambers to slow their aging – otherwise they will be old before they arrive at their new world.

The cylinders clustered around the ramjet's body carry the colonists, tools and supplies they will need.

The delta-winged spaceplane will be used to explore the target planet.

How it works

The ramjet's generators (**1**) produce a giant magnetic field up to 4,800km (3,000 miles) across (**2**) that sucks in hydrogen atoms in the ship's path. These are fed into a nuclear reactor (**3**) which spews out a radio active exhaust (**4**) that drives the craft at a speed approaching 300,000km (186,000 miles) per second.

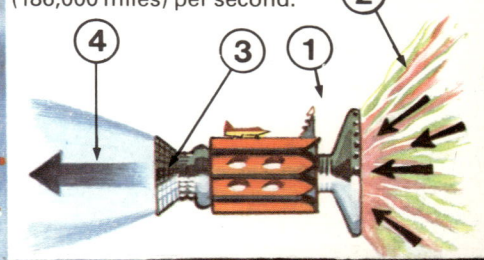

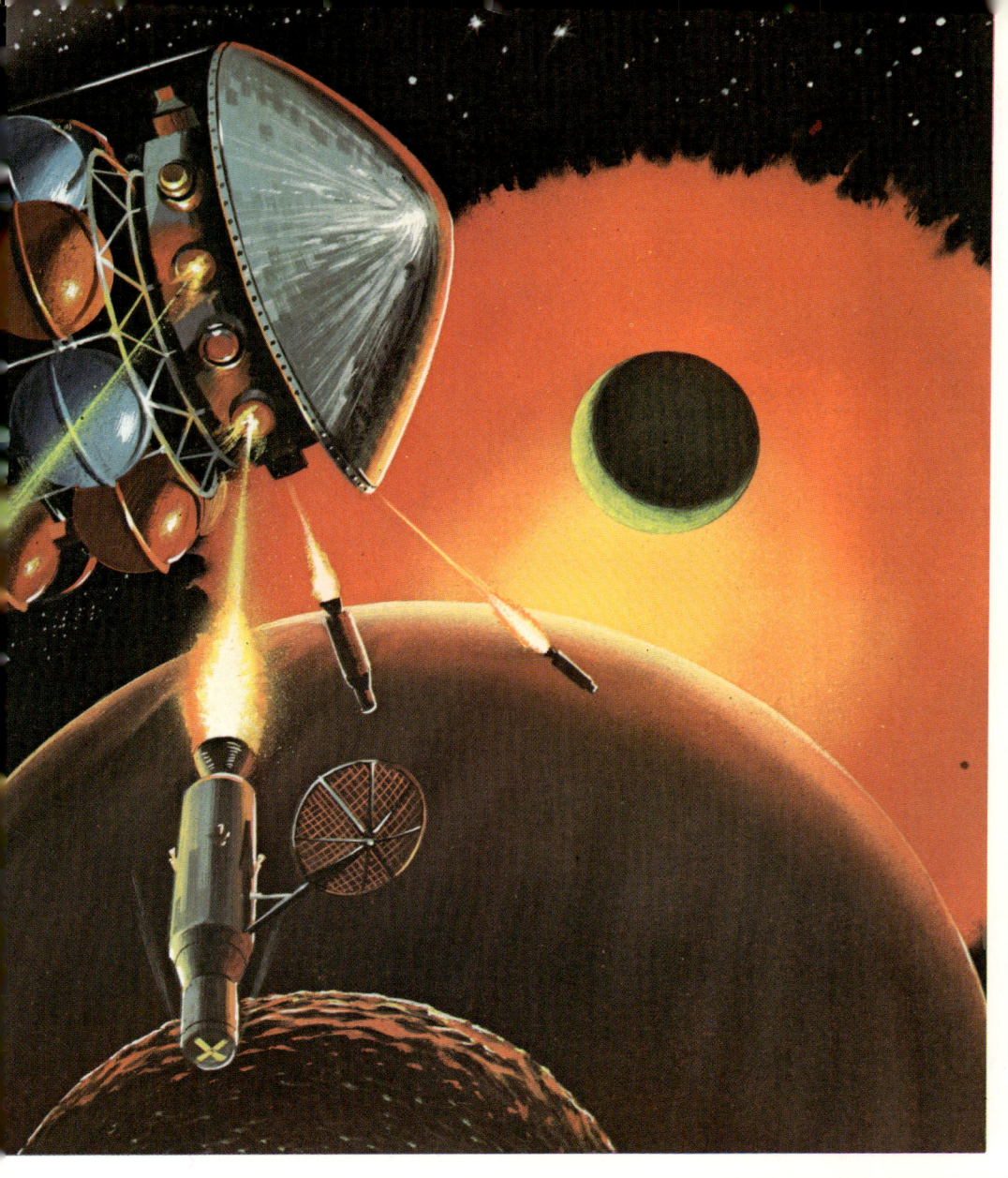

Starprobe mission profile

Earth's first unmanned starprobe flies past a planet close to Barnard's Star, six light-years from the Sun. The red star casts a fierce glow over the planet and its two moons.

The probe has been travelling for 49 years, guided by a computer that adjusts the various systems and directs necessary repairs. Spherical tanks ring the craft. They provide fuel for the second-stage engine, used for course corrections during the flight.

Smaller probes are shown leaving the parent ship to explore the planet. Their findings will be automatically radioed back to the computer.

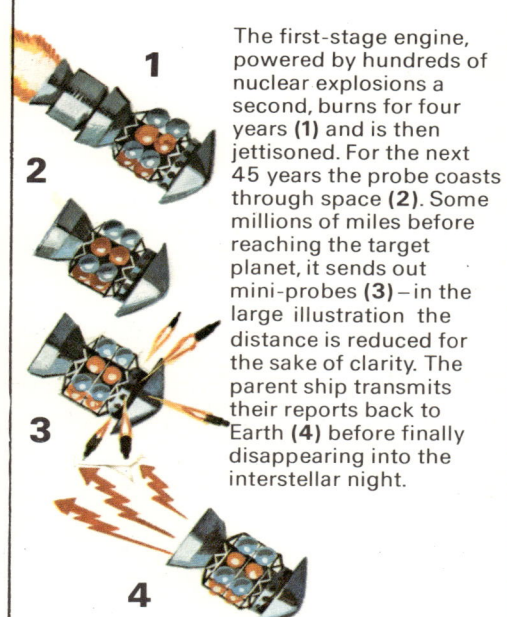

1 The first-stage engine, powered by hundreds of nuclear explosions a second, burns for four years (1) and is then jettisoned. For the next 45 years the probe coasts through space (2). Some millions of miles before reaching the target planet, it sends out mini-probes (3) – in the large illustration the distance is reduced for the sake of clarity. The parent ship transmits their reports back to Earth (4) before finally disappearing into the interstellar night.

ALIEN LIFE

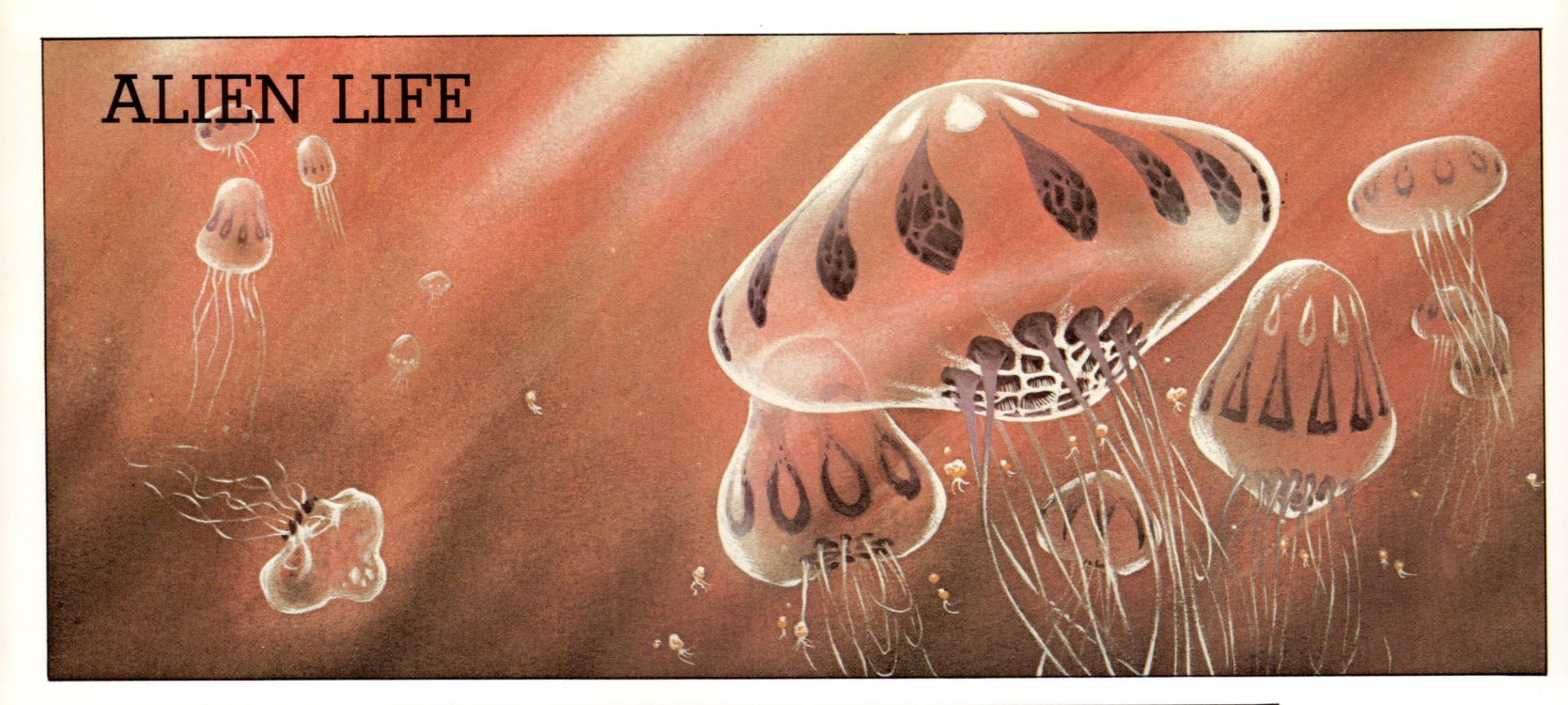

▲ **A colony of** balloon-like creatures float through the hydrogen clouds of a Jupiter-like world. They move by expanding and contracting a gas-filled sack in their bodies. The tentacles are used for gathering food. At left, an ageing creature that has lost control of its gas-sack sinks slowly to the depths.

◀ **A crab-like creature** ventures out into the fierce light of a planet orbiting the double star Beta Lyrae. A fan-like shell protects it from heat and radiation. It has two pairs of eyes – the large ones for use in the deep shadows of its world, and a small pair for squinting into the glare of daylight.

▲ **The Universe** is so big that most scientists now believe that life of some kind must exist elsewhere in it. Some of the weird and wonderful life forms that could have developed on other worlds are shown here.

If we go to the stars we can expect to find life there. Of course it is just possible that we shan't. The evolution of life on Earth may be unique. Or there may not be Earth-sized planets suitable for life anywhere else in the Universe. But scientists prefer to think it more likely that there are other planets circling other stars. And they think that life may be possible on at least some of them.

The chances of life in space

Star travellers may not find life on planets round the nearer stars. But we can assume that it will be found somewhere in our Galaxy. We know that the whole Universe is made up of the same atoms. Among so many stars – ten thousand million million million of them, made of the same atoms as our Solar System – we are not likely to be unique.

From working out sums like this, scientists have come to the conclusion that there may be as many as a million technological civilizations in the Galaxy. But by the same sums the nearest must be several hundred light-years away.

Life past, present and to come

These figures are for technological civilizations in existence now. To that number should be added other millions for the civilizations that have been destroyed or have yet to come into existence. After all, we have only had civilization on this planet for a few thousand years.

There is no reason to think that the inhabitants of other planets will look like humans. This is very unlikely. Humans have taken millions of years to look as they do now. We might have turned out very differently if conditions on the planet had been slightly altered.

The way we have evolved has been decided by two main factors – Earth's gravity and its atmosphere.

On a bigger planet gravity would be stronger. If other conditions were like ours, there might be a human type of life. But the 'aliens' would be shorter and heavier than us. (Alien means foreign, and is often used to describe life on another planet. Another term used is 'extra-terrestrial', which means coming from outside Earth.) On a smaller planet they would be taller and lighter.

Creatures from other atmospheres

Earth's atmosphere is made up of nitrogen and oxygen, mixed with other elements. This is what human beings and animals need to breathe. But other planets might be quite different. Their inhabitants

▲ **A frog-like amphibian** surveys its city from a transporter platform. Its eyes, set on protected swivels, give it all-round vision – a big evolutionary advantage in the swamps and marshes of its world. Webbed feet enable it to hunt under water, while its unwebbed fingers can handle tools like the dart-gun on its belt.

The amphibians have a technological civilization. Their bubble-dome city is built on two levels: machinery is kept above the surface, while comfortable living-quarters lie below in the warm, watery depths.

▲ **A Cyborg** (cybernetic organism) glides over a desert world orbiting Proxima Centauri. This race of intelligent machines began evolving when a brain was transplanted into a robot. A revolving head-unit provides information about the creature's surroundings.

▲ **Man himself may take charge** of his own evolution by pioneering the use of personal computer inputs. These could provide two-way communication with a 'university satellite' that would provide instant information and serve as a collective memory.

might not be able to live in our atmosphere, and men might die in theirs.

A different atmosphere would cause a different pressure on the body too. This would affect its size, shape and strength. On some planets life may have evolved under a pressure that would crush a man on Earth.

Our atmosphere also allows us to see through very small eyes. The light waves we use can travel very fast. They can be concentrated, so that the receiver, the eye, can be a very small one. On other planets other sorts of waves might have to be used – radio waves, perhaps. The receiver would then have to be very large.

Worlds under water

Two-thirds of the Earth is sea. Man evolved from animals that once lived in the sea. But he developed his civilization on land. On another planet there might be intelligent life, perhaps even a technological civilization, still in the water. There is evidence on Earth that this might be possible. Dolphins and whales have no arms and so can't make the tools needed for a technological civilization. But they have a brain capacity as large as that of humans

A different pace of life

Another way in which aliens may be different from us is in their life-span and speed of living.

Human beings live at a certain speed. They convert food into energy at a certain rate. Their bodies grow from birth and then decay till death. Their average life-span is about 60 to 70 years. But other animals on Earth live at different rates. Most of them, such as insects, live at a faster rate and die earlier. A few such as giant tortoises live longer than men.

Alien life-forms may vary in the same way. Some aliens may have extremely long life-spans. To them men may seem as hurried in their movements as humming-birds or ants seem to us on Earth.

By the time our descendants meet alien life our species may have evolved beyond the point we are at today. Our bodies may have changed physically. We may have lost all our hair, and perhaps our teeth. People born and brought up free of Earth's gravity – on a space station, for example – will be even more different physically. Their bodies will be thinner and their bones more delicate.

Machine men

It is possible that men will also evolve so that they can use machines as extensions of their bodies. Our descendants would then just plug into computers and memory banks. The human brain would then be very much more powerful. Human beings would be able to do things we can only dream of today.

HOLE IN SPACE TEST

THE FAR FUTURE

Scientists can't see the whole of the Universe. It is too big. But from what they have seen they know that the basic laws of physics are the same for the whole Universe.

One of these laws is very important for men who dream of travelling vast distances in space. This is the law that nothing that has mass can travel faster than light.

When time slows down

This is part of what is called the 'theory of relativity', discovered by Einstein in the early years of this century. One of its effects is that time appears to slow down the nearer one gets to the speed of light.

If a man travelled to the stars at a speed close to that of light, time would seem to go more slowly on his spacecraft, than for an observer on Earth. If he returned to Earth he would be only a few years older than he was when he left. But the Earth itself would have aged by hundreds of thousands of years.

Another effect of relativity is that the mass of the spaceship would increase with its speed. The nearer it went to the speed of light the more massive it would become, and the bigger its engines would need to be.

Space empires?

In the future men might want to set up an empire in space. But from what is now known they seem unlikely to succeed. Spaceships might be built to travel near the speed of light. But they would be useless for the sort of communication between worlds which would make a central government possible.

For the same reasons it would be difficult to communicate with the neighbouring stars in the Galaxy. But some scientists now think that there may be a way to travel faster than light. These scientists do not dispute the facts of relativity. But they say there may be 'holes' in space and time.

Short cuts through space

Science fiction writers have speculated that these holes might make it possible to travel from one part of space and time to another in, quite literally, no time at all. They would be short cuts through space.

One way of understanding how these holes might work is to imagine that the two 'stars' at the top of these pages are hundreds of light years apart. Close the

HOLE IN SPACE TEST

▲ **An interstellar battlecraft** fights off a laser attack in a battle of the distant future. Now the speculations of scientists are outpacing the wildest fantasies of science fiction writers. Could objects passing through the space whirlpools called black holes re-emerge in another place and time? The picture (right) imagines a spacecraft generating a protective field to enter one without being torn apart.

pages and the stars are next to each other. Some people think that the holes in space would have the same effect.

Although scientists believe they exist, they have never seen these holes.

Collapsing stars

When a star burns up all its fuel it starts to collapse on itself, like a deflating balloon. This is because of the force of gravity. It eventually collapses until it is very small. But what is left has a very large mass. It is so dense that a tiny piece of it could weigh a million tonnes (tons).

Scientists call these collapsed stars 'neutron stars'. Spinning neutron stars give out radio waves which astronomers can detect.

A star which started with a mass which was very much larger than that of the Sun would go on collapsing beyond neutron star state. The force of gravity would become greater and greater. Eventually it would become so great and the mass so dense that even light would not be able to escape. The star would then disappear from view. These phenomena have been called 'black holes'.

The neutron stars and black holes make scientists think that there are 'holes' in the space-time continuum. They reason that the matter in the Universe – everything that exists – cannot disappear in any real sense. It must go somewhere, so it appears somewhere else, possibly in another part of the Universe.

Faster than light

Scientists believe that these holes exist. It is obviously too soon to be sure that they can be used as short cuts through time and space. If they could, though, there would be a way of getting round the constant law of the Universe – that nobody can travel faster than light.

▲ **In science fiction,** they now talk about hyperspace, in which the known laws of the Universe do not apply. Could a network of black and white holes be the entry and exit points of another Universe?

27

INDEX

Aldebaran, 4
Aldrin, Edwin, 9,16
alien life, 24-25
Alpha Centauri, 6
Andromeda, 6
animal astronauts, 11
Apollo, 16, 22
Arecibo radio telescope, 8-9
Armstrong, Neil, 9,16
Asteroid Belt, 2,5
asteroids, 4,5,21,22
autopilot, 22

backpack, 12
balloon-like creatures, 24
Barnard's Star 22,23
Betelgeuse, 6
black holes, 27
Brahe, Tycho, 8

Centaurus, 6
Ceres, 5
Challenger, space
    shuttle, 16
clothing, 12-13
collapsing stars, 27
colonies on the stars, 22
comets, 4,5
constant law of the Universe,
    26-27
Copernicus, 8,16
crab-like creatures, 24
Cyborg, 25
61 Cygni, 22

Dog Star, 6,22
double stars, 6
dwarf stars, 6

Earth, 4,5,7
Einstein, 26
engines, 22
Epsilon Eridani, 22
Epsilon Indi, 22
evolution of life, 24
Explorer 1, 9,16
extra-terrestrial, 24

frog-like amphibian, 25

Gagarin, Yuri, 9,16
galaxies, 6,7
Galileo, 8,16
Ganymede, 5
Glenn, John, 16
Goddard, Robert H., 8
gravity, 7

Halley's comet, 16
heatshield, 10-11
helmet, 12,13
Herschel, 8
hole in space test, 26,27
hydrogen, 22
hyperspace, 27

interstellar battlecraft, 27

Jupiter, 4,5

Kepler, Johannes, 8,16
Kvant module, 16

Leonov, 16
life in space, 24-25
light-years, 6,7,22
Luna 1, 10
Luna 9, 9,10
Luna 16, 10
Luna orbiters, 10
Lunokhod, 10,11
Luyters 726-8, 22

machine men, 25
Magellanic Clouds, 6
mapping the planets, 10
Mariner 4, 16
Mariner 9, 10, 11
Mariner 10, 4, 10, 16
Mars, 4,5
Mercury, 4
Milky Way, 6,7
minerals, 21
Mir space station, 14, 16
MMU (Manned
    Manoeuvring Unit), 13
Moon, 9
moonliner, 21
moon-mining, 21
moons, 4,5
multi-generation expedition, 22

Neptune, 4,5
neutron stars, 27
Newton, Sir Isaac, 7,8,16

optical telescopes, 9
Orion, 6

photographing the planets, 10
photons, 22
photosphere, 4
Pioneer 10, 9,10,16
Pioneer 11, 9,10
Pluto, 4,5,8,16
portable life support system, 13
pressure suits, 12-13
prominences, 5
Proxima Centauri, 6,22

radio telescope, 8
ramjet, 22-23
Ranger 7, 10
red giant star, 6
reflector telescope, 8
refuelling in space, 22
rings, 4
robot explorers, 9,10-11
robot work-force, 21

satellites, artificial, 9,14,16
Saturn, 4,5
Sirius, 6,22
Skylab, 16
solar cells, 25

solar panels, 11
Solar System, 4,5,7
solar flares, 16
Soyuz, 16
space cities, 15
Spacelab, 14
space probes, 9
Space Race, 9
space rockets, 8
space shuttle, 14-15,16
space stations, 14
space suits, 12-13
Space Telescope, 14
space travel, 22-23
spectroscope, 8
Sputnik 1, 9,16
starprobe, 23
stars 6-7
starships, 22-23
Sun, 4,6,22
sun spots, 4
Surveyor 3, 11

Tau Ceti, 22
technological civilization, 25
telescopes, 8,9
temperatures of stars, 6
Tereshkova, Valentina, 16
theory of relativity, 26
timechart, 16
Titan, 5

Universe, 6
unmanned craft, 10-11
Uranus, 4,5

Venera, 10,11,16
Venus, 4,10,11
Viking, 11,16
von Braun, Wernher, 9
Voyagers 1 & 2, 4, 10, 11, 16

Wolf 359, 22